He's My

Brother

He's My Brother

Former Racial Foes Offer Strategy
for Reconciliation

John Perkins and
Thomas A. Tarrants, III
with
David Wimbish

Chosen Books
A Division of Baker Book House Co
Grand Rapids, Michigan 49516

© 1994 by John Perkins and Thomas A. Tarrants, III

Published by Chosen Books
a division of Baker Book House Company
P.O. Box 6287, Grand Rapids, MI 49516-6287

Second printing, May 1995

Printed in the United States of America

Library of Congress Cataloging-in-Publication Data

Perkins, John, 1930–
    He's my brother: former racial foes offer strategy for reconciliation / John
Perkins and Thomas A. Tarrants, III, with David Wimbish.
    p. cm.
    ISBN 0-8007-9214-9
    1. Racism—United States. 2. Racism—Mississippi. 3. United States—Race
relations. 4. Mississippi—Race relations. 5. Race relations—Religious
aspects—Christianity. I. Tarrants, Thomas A. II. Wimbish, David. III. Title.
E185.615.P42   1994
305.8'00973—dc20   94-4075

Unless otherwise noted, Scripture passages quoted by John Perkins or identified NKJV are from The New King James Version. Copyright © 1979, 1980, 1982, Thomas Nelson, Inc., Publishers.

Scripture texts quoted by Thomas A. Tarrants, III, or identified NIV are from the HOLY BIBLE, NEW INTERNATIONAL VERSION®. NIV®. Copyright © 1973, 1978, 1984 International Bible Society. Used by permission of Zondervan Publishing House.

Scripture texts identified KJV are from the King James Version.

Contents

Introduction   7

Part 1 Soldiers in a War   11
  1 Los Angeles Is Burning   13
  2 To Be Young, American . . . and Black   26
  3 How I Learned to Hate   37

Part 2 Hearts Aflame   51
  4 Into the Fire   53
  5 War!   74
  6 Into the Maelstrom   84
  7 45 Minutes to Live   105
  8 A Conversion of Love   129
  9 Thank God Almighty, I'm Free at Last!   134
  10 Living in the Light   139

Part 3 Developing a Strategy for Reconciliation   157
  11 The Model for Reconciliation   159
  12 But What Can I Do About It?   174
  13 Heeding the Call to Reconciliation   192
  14 Relearning the Three R's   222
  15 A Final Word   231

All royalties from the sale of this book are being donated to the John Perkins Foundation to further the work of racial reconciliation and Christian community development in the U.S.

Introduction

Tom Tarrants thought of himself as a soldier in a war against a Communist conspiracy that was threatening to destroy the United States. That conspiracy involved such preposterous notions as the belief that blacks should have equal protection under the law, that they should be accorded the same respect, privileges and opportunities enjoyed by white Americans.

Tarrants was willing to fight in order to stop the individuals he believed were intent on bringing America to her knees. In order to survive, he believed, America must be pure and steadfast and, most of all, white. Ultimately Tarrants' war against the conspiracy came to a halt amidst a hail of bullets in Meridian, Mississippi.

It was in a Mississippi prison cell, on death row, that Tarrants began to read a book that changed first his views, then his whole life. That book was the Bible.

One verse in particular blasted its way into his consciousness: "For what shall it profit a man, if he shall gain the whole world, and lose his own soul?" (Mark 8:36 KJV). That verse drove him to his knees, where he experienced a life-changing encounter with the risen Lord of the universe.

John Perkins was a soldier in a different kind of war. His was a battle against poverty and injustice. It involved taking the Gospel back to the poor black residents of his native Mississippi. He believed that the Gospel had much to say not only about the immortal souls of men, but about their physical welfare as well.

John Perkins believed that the Gospel was intended to "set the captives free," and that meant helping Mississippi's poor blacks find a way to overcome the poverty that had ground them down for many years. It meant finding a way to improve the substandard housing that was prevalent throughout the black community; assisting in the fight for equal justice under the law; helping blacks register to vote so they could have a fair say in the shaping of their communities.

When Perkins first began to feel that God was calling him away from his adopted California and back to Mississippi, his wife was adamantly opposed. Vera Mae knew what life was like in those days for blacks in the deep South. Like her husband, she had grown up in Mississippi. She had been glad when she was finally able to leave that state behind her, and the only way she would think about going back was to visit her family.

But her husband knew the call of God and would not be dissuaded.

John Perkins ran into resistance in Mississippi, as he knew he would. He received telephone threats in the middle of the night and hate-filled Ku Klux Klan material mailed anonymously. But he never really feared for his safety, because he knew beyond any doubt, under the conviction of the Holy Spirit, that he was doing what God had called him to do.

Then one night in the little town of Brandon, some white men wearing police uniforms decided to teach this "uppity nigger" a lesson. Only a man intimately acquainted with God could have endured such savage treatment and continued to persevere toward the goal to which he had been called.

Today Tom Tarrants and John Perkins still bear the scars of the injuries they received while they were fighting on opposite sides of the battle for racial equality. Today they are fighting on the same side, having joined in a battle of hope and love waged against forces and attitudes that threaten to tear this country apart.

Both men are committed to what they are doing. Both know beyond a doubt that they are being led by the Holy Spirit. And both know that racism and anger between the races is much more than a social issue. It is a spiritual issue that can be resolved only through reconciliation brought about by the redeeming blood of Jesus Christ.

God is calling His people, they believe, to be actively involved in bringing about that reconciliation. Nothing is more important to the welfare of the United States, they know, than that people of all races learn to work together to overcome racism and bigotry. They look around them today and see an America teetering on the verge of a race war. They also see a Church fragmented and stunted by segregation and isolation of different racial and ethnic groups. Our divisions are holding us back. They are a hindrance to the furtherance of the Gospel—and God the Father weeps because of it.

John Perkins and Tom Tarrants know that the race-related riots that tore apart south-central Los Angeles during the spring of 1992 were only one symptom of a deeper problem.

In this book they will tell their stories. They will also present a workable strategy aimed at building bridges of understanding and reconciliation between the races.

Now.

While there is still time to avert disaster.

Part 1

Soldiers in a War

Los Angeles Is Burning

Tom Tarrants

Sunday, June 30, 1968, Meridian, Mississippi

This was going to be easy—a piece of cake.

We would get in, plant the bomb and be miles down the road by the time the explosion shattered the Mississippi darkness. Even if something unusual did happen, I was prepared. A fully loaded nine-millimeter Browning automatic pistol sat on the seat beside me, and I had a submachine gun and hand grenade under the seat. I was ready for war.

There was no doubt in my mind that we were in a war. After all, I was a soldier—a soldier in the war against the Jews and blacks who were tearing apart the country I loved. All the talk about civil rights and equality was nothing more than a smokescreen for their real aim: to weaken the United States to the point that she would be unable to resist her Communist enemies and their Jewish masters.

It was almost time now. Everything was going according to plan. As I turned the corner onto 29th Avenue, it was nearly

13

12:45 A.M. and everything seemed perfect. The neighborhood was dark—no one out walking, no cars, no dogs barking. This one was going to be easy.

I glanced over at my partner, my friend who sat beside me, and thought how much she did *not* look like a fighter. At 26, Kathy Ainsworth was five years older than I. She was an attractive young woman—a petite brunette with big brown eyes and almost perfect skin. She looked fragile, like a little girl's favorite doll. But she had the heart and nerves of a seasoned terrorist.

Kathy was an elementary schoolteacher by day—a gentle, kind woman who loved the children she taught. Always polite, putting a sir or ma'am onto the end of a sentence, she was a perfect Southern lady. She did not look like the sort of woman who would carry a pistol in her handbag or be getting ready to blow up a trouble-making Jewish leader.

But Kathy, like me, hated the Jews and blacks for what they were doing to our country. And the focal point of her hatred (as it was of mine) was the Jewish conspirators who were using the blacks for their own anti-American purposes.

We hated them because they had made us go to school with blacks, forced us to open up our neighborhoods to them and allow them to eat in our restaurants. Most of all we hated them because we knew what they were really up to. And now the South was full of them—agitators from the North who were stirring up trouble and trying to change the way we had done things for hundreds of years. I hated them with a passion.

I noticed that Kathy's pretty face did not betray a hint of nervousness or fear. She was calm and collected. In fact, if any emotion at all showed in her eyes, it was determination.

Our target lay just ahead—the home of Meyer Davidson, a Jewish businessman who had spoken out strongly in favor of the civil rights movement and denounced the Ku Klux Klan. I looked down at the box full of dynamite that sat on the front seat between us. The timer was set for 2:00 A.M., which meant that by the time the house was reduced to a pile of rubble, Kathy and I would be thirty miles or more down the road to Miami.

As I drove up slowly to our target, I switched off the lights and let the car coast down the hill toward the Davidsons' house. I pulled over and parked beneath a towering oak tree. This was it.

I opened the car door, put my pistol in my belt, took the bomb and began to walk up the driveway toward the carport.

I had not made it very far when a gunshot rang out in the darkness, then an indistinguishable shout, followed by more shots.

Kathy and I had walked into a trap.

Police sharpshooters were staked out in the yards adjacent to the house, and a team was sitting on the embankment of the lawn directly across the street, just a few yards from where we had parked the car.

I dropped the bomb and spun around to run. As I turned, my pistol fell out of my waistband, and I ran as fast as I could for the car, not realizing I was running directly into the police gunfire. It was a miracle the bomb did not explode. If it had, it would have blown us all sky-high.

Just as I got to the car amid a hail of gunfire, I felt the hard jolt of a shotgun blast in the upper part of my right leg. Stunned, I struggled to the driver's door. Kathy tried frantically to help me get inside.

Bullets seemed to be coming at us from everywhere. No sooner had I made it into the car than another policeman's bullet tore into Kathy's neck.

"Tommy," she said, "I've been hit."

Then she fell back against the front seat of the car and was quiet.

I did not know if she was dead or alive, but I did know blood was pouring out of both of us and that I had to get us out of there. Somehow, amid continued gunfire and the sound of bullets ripping into our Buick, I managed to start the ignition. Jamming the accelerator to the floor, I tore off down 29th Avenue.

But when I looked into my rear-view mirror, I could see that a patrol car was in hot pursuit. Then I saw a cop leaning out the passenger window.

Boom!

I was showered with bits of broken glass as the back window of the Buick was shattered by the blast from his gun.

And he kept firing.

The wound in my leg was massive. Blood was pouring out. But I was going on adrenaline. Kathy, who now lay crumpled half on the seat and half on the floor, was not moving, probably dead. I had to shake these guys and get back to Jackson and a doctor.

My tires squealed as I swerved right onto 21st Street, then took another right, then a left. The police car stayed right behind me, the cop blasting away. Finally he hit my tires. As I skidded to a stop, the patrol car rammed me from behind, bouncing our Buick into a fire hydrant and slamming me against the steering wheel.

But I still was not ready to surrender.

More by instinct than design, I grabbed my submachine gun, jumped out of the car and began firing bursts in the direction of the patrol car.

The officer on the passenger side pushed his door open and aimed his shotgun at me. I blasted him before he could get off another shot, and he fell to the ground.

When my clip emptied, the other cop, who had ducked beneath the dashboard, jumped up and fired, hitting me in the upper part of my left leg.

I do not know how I managed to stay on my feet, but somehow I ran across the street and into the backyard of the corner house, moving as fast as I could while dragging my right leg.

Behind me I heard shouts, the pounding of heavy footsteps, the click of weapons being reloaded. It seemed that every cop in the world was after me.

Surrounding the yard was a chain-link fence, partially concealed by shrubbery. Maybe, just maybe if I could get over that fence, I could get away. I was in agony from my bullet wounds, but this was life or death.

But as I grabbed the top of the fence, a surge of searing pain shot through my body and sent me sprawling to the ground. The top of the fence was electrified! I fell into a clump of bushes and—exhausted and nearly dead from pain and loss of blood—had no choice but to lie there gushing blood and feeling my life ebbing away.

Minutes later, several policemen with flashlights spotted me. Slowly, cautiously, they approached with their guns trained on me. Then, when they were almost over me, they turned off their lights and opened fire.

Two of the blasts tore into my right arm, nearly severing it, and I knew I was going to die. In my semi-conscious state, I sensed that someone was shining a flashlight in my face and I heard a voice ask, "Is he dead?"

"No," someone answered. "The son of a bitch is still alive."

"Shoot him! Shoot him!"

"No! No! Don't shoot! The neighbors are here!"

A minute or so later, an ambulance driver rushed up and I was loaded onto a stretcher. Near the ambulance I heard a dispassionate voice say, "The woman is dead, and this one isn't going to make it."

My days as a terrorist had finally come to an end.

What I did not know was that God had just intervened in my life.

It is painful for me, looking back on it now, to realize how full of bitterness and violence I was. God had to render me—like many stubborn men and women—totally helpless before He could get my attention.

But by the grace of God, the Holy Spirit was about to turn my life around.

John Perkins

Saturday, February 7, 1970, Mendenhall, Mississippi

It was just after sundown when we got the phone call.

Louise Fox, one of our Voice of Calvary workers, was on the line, telling us that a group of our college students had been arrested without apparent reason. They had been booked into the Rankin County Jail in Brandon, and she was worried about their safety.

I assured her I would get there as soon as I could. I hung up the phone, grabbed my coat and told Vera Mae I had important business to attend to, but that I would be back just as soon as I could. I also breathed a prayer, asking God to protect these fine young men and women and let them know He was there with them, no matter what they might be facing.

The truth was, I was afraid for these college students who had been arrested, even though I tried to give Vera Mae the idea it was no big deal. Of course, she knew better.

I knew these college students could be in big trouble because they had been with us in Mendenhall that day, helping us in our efforts to bring economic equality and justice to this small Southern town. To put it as clearly as possible, they were taking part in activities that would not endear them to law enforcement personnel within the state of Mississippi.

We had been making our feelings known by protesting, marching and singing our anthem of the day: "Do right, white man, do right." Mendenhall was like a lot of other little Southern towns in that we were forced to live on the edge of the economy. We had always had to survive on whatever crumbs the white community was willing to toss us. But now we were insisting that things had to change. We were asking for no special favors or considerations. We wanted only what was fair.

So those of us at Voice of Calvary Ministries, along with a few hundred people from Mendenhall and the surrounding counties and helped along by a goodly number of students from Tougaloo College in Jackson, were trying to make enough of a stir that things would actually begin to change.

As we had marched, sung and protested that day, the streets of Mendenhall had been lined with law enforcement officials from city, county and state agencies. We had seen white policemen with their nightsticks in their hands, some of them looking like they were itching to bust open a black head or two. We saw white Highway Patrolmen wearing gas masks just in case they had to use tear gas to get us to disperse. And we had seen white sheriff's officers with their shotguns loaded and ready for action. There had been hundreds of white onlookers, of course, some of whom shouted obscenities and racial slurs at us.

Some of the white folks looking on may have agreed with us. Some of them may even have wanted to join us. But they didn't. If they felt the least bit of support for what we were doing, they did not show it. Except for a few white college students who had come from outside the state to help us, we were a small island of blacks in a sea of angry whites.

We knew that a lot of folks in town did not like what we were saying, but we also knew they were hearing us. That was a victory of sorts. We tried to let them know we were not looking for a confrontation. We were not interested in violence or revenge. We made sure everybody knew we were Christians, brothers and sisters in Christ. Our protest marches always included prayers and hymns, and we invited our white Christian "brethren" to join us— although none did.

More than a few of them had been shocked and surprised by what was going on in Mendenhall. More than one white onlooker had spotted the son or daughter of his maid or gardener in our ranks and yelled out that he was going to tell the parent about the child's participation in the march. Many of the white people there had never tried to look past the stereotype of the shuffling, smiling, happy-go-lucky colored person—and they were astonished when we began to speak out loudly for equality and justice. They had never suspected anything was wrong. Why, they figured they treated us pretty good, and that we must be deliriously happy about it.

They did not have a clue as to what life was really like for most of the black citizens of Mendenhall . . . of Mississippi . . . of the United States of America.

But, like I said, it had been a relatively peaceful day in spite of all the potential for trouble. I think we were all feeling pretty good about things by the time the college students piled into their two vans and headed out of Mendenhall on Highway 49 on their way back to Jackson. Before they left that day, in fact, we gathered back at the Voice of Calvary to praise and thank Jesus for His guidance and protection during the day. Then they piled into the two vehicles that were to take them back to college.

Most of the students—nineteen of them, in fact—were riding in a Dodge van being driven by a bright young man named Doug Huemmer. The rest of them followed in a just-as-crowded Volkswagen bus driven by Louise Fox. Doug and Louise were whites who had come from outside the area to help our cause.

Just outside the little town of Plain, as I heard Doug tell it later, he looked into his rear-view mirror and saw a Mississippi Highway Patrol car coming up behind him. It maneuvered around the Volkswagen and pulled in behind the Dodge. As soon as it got between the two vans, the patrolman turned on his siren and his flashing blue lights.

Doug remembers saying something like, "I don't like the looks of this."

It was an empty stretch of highway. There were no businesses or houses, nor was there much in the way of traffic. If the authorities wanted to beat up a few niggers or a white troublemaker, this was a good place to do it.

Doug waved out the window for the other van to go on. No sense everyone getting into trouble, he figured. But Louise was not about to leave her friends behind, so after driving a little farther down the highway, she, too, pulled off the road to see what was going to happen.

A patrolman, Douglas O. Baldwin, got out of his car, strode up to the driver's window of the Dodge van and ordered Doug to get out. Doug knew better than to resist or even hesitate. He did what he was told immediately.

Baldwin ordered Doug into his patrol car, where he told him he had been stopped because he had almost had a head-on collision with a pickup truck.

Doug replied, as politely as possible, that he did not see how that could have been possible, especially because he had been driving in the right-hand lane of a four-lane highway.

But Patrolman Baldwin changed the subject quickly. "Are you some of the demonstrators from Mendenhall?"

Doug answered that they were.

"Well, I'm sick and tired of this civil rights stuff," Baldwin told him, "and we're not going to take it anymore."

Staring angrily at the mixture of young black and white faces peering out the rear windows of the Dodge van, Patrolman Baldwin got on his radio and asked for backup.

Exactly what he said is open for debate. Doug remembers it as something like, "I've got a bunch of niggers and some whites down here. They're armed, and I need some help to clean them out."

"What's going on?" Doug asked the patrolman. "Am I being charged with a traffic violation?"

"Shut up," Baldwin replied, "or I'll shoot you in the head."

He put his hand on his sidearm to show he meant business.

In a matter of minutes, four or five more patrol cars arrived on the scene, sirens wailing and lights flashing. Emerging from their cars with weapons drawn, the officers ordered everyone out of the van.

In the late afternoon mist, the nineteen students were lined up against the van, frisked and handcuffed. All the while, most of the patrolmen kept up a steady stream of derogatory comments, cursing, damning and threatening the students. They were probably hoping to provoke a reaction—a little bit of resisting arrest—to give them an excuse to do some head-bashing.

When the students failed to react in any way, the patrolmen merely herded them into the various patrol cars for transportation to the Brandon jail. As soon as the cars drove away, Louise Fox drove fast to the town of Plain, where she stopped at the first pay phone she saw, called me and told me what was going on.

Good friends Curry Brown and Joe Paul Buckley rode along with me to Brandon. While we were on our way, the students were being booked into the jail on a variety of charges ranging from "reckless driving" to "carrying a concealed brick." Only later did I find out that as they were being booked, they were being kicked and beaten with billy clubs.

Even without knowing this, I was angry. But I figured that as soon as we got to Brandon, we would be able to post bail for these kids, and that would be that—at least for a while. The Highway Patrol had made its point loud and clear.

It never occurred to me to question why the patrolmen had arrested everyone in Doug's van and let Louise and her van full of college students continue on its way unmolested. I never thought that those patrolmen knew she would call me—the one who was "causing" all the trouble—or that they knew I would come. It never dawned on me, even for a moment, that I would be walking into a trap that would nearly cost me my life.

But before that long night was over, I was beaten, kicked, stomped into unconsciousness and revived just so I could be beaten unconscious once again. And all of this by men—white men—wearing the uniforms and badges of the Mississippi Highway Patrol and the Rankin County Sheriff's Department.

As they beat me, they kept saying it over and over: "Nigger! Take that, nigger!"

I cannot remember everything that happened that night. I do remember seeing blood all over the floor and realizing that most of it had come from me. Not all of it, though. The other men were being beaten, too, as were some of the students.

In between beating us, these men who were sworn to uphold the law made me get down on my hands and knees and wipe up the blood, yelling at me for getting their nice, clean floor all dirty. Someone said that the FBI was coming over to see what was going on, and the local boys certainly did not want the FBI to find their floor covered with blood!

I thought that night would go on forever, or at least that I would not be alive when it finally ended. I really do not know, looking back on it now, how I survived. God's hand was certainly upon me.

I was beaten all over my head. They blackened my eyes. They kicked me in the stomach. They beat me on my back and shoulders.

But they did not kill me.

Finally they flung me into a cell.

The college students who shared that cell with me watched over me through the rest of the night, doing whatever they could to help. Mostly that meant soaking a shirt in cold water and applying it to one of my injuries. I never knew or asked where they got the cold water. All I knew, as I drifted in and out of consciousness, was that my life would never be the same.

I knew then, more than I had ever known before, the potential for evil within the human heart. I knew the depth of hatred one man can feel for another, simply because his skin is not the same color. If I had had any illusions before, I certainly had none now. I knew that the battle to make this country a place where there really is "liberty and justice for all" was going to be long and tough.

Tom Tarrants

Sunday, March 29, 1992, Los Angeles

The city was burning.

Or at least large portions of it were—especially in the south central part of the city, an area whose population is heavily black and Hispanic.

I was not there, but I saw it on television, along with millions of people across the country. We watched in horror as building after building was torched by angry mobs; as looters smashed the windows of stores and emptied them of merchandise; as people who tried to stop the rioting and looting were beaten; as some looters were shot dead by store-owners trying to protect their property. We watched as innocent men, who happened to be in the wrong place at the wrong time, were attacked and beaten mercilessly.

Some of us fell to our knees in prayer over what was happening. We prayed for the victims of the rioting and looting, and in compassion for the ones who were involved in the violence. And some of us prayed earnestly—in agony, even—regarding the underlying attitudes and cirumstances that brought about this madness. We prayed that God would help us find the way to understanding and reconciliation between the races.

When the fires were finally extinguished and the smoke had cleared, more than fifty people were dead and $45 billion worth of property had been destroyed. Hundreds of business owners had been wiped out, and many of them were Korean, Hispanic or black.

Can such an event happen again? It can—it might—unless we all work together, in the name and power of Jesus, to change things.

John Perkins

Sunday, March 29, 1992, Los Angeles

We all know what started the Los Angeles riots.

I am pretty sure there is not a person in this country who has not seen at least twice the videotape of the beating of Rodney King by the Los Angeles Police Department. We all saw how the police officers continued to hit him with their batons even though he was already lying prostrate on the ground. That did not touch off any rioting.

But now a nearly all-white jury had ruled that the policemen had done nothing wrong, that they had used "reasonable force" in subduing King after a high-speed chase.

Almost as soon as the verdict was in, the black community in Los Angeles erupted in a frenzy of frustration, violence and destruction that nearly became an all-out race war.

To black Americans, what happened to Rodney King was an old, old story. The same is true of the verdict that found the policemen not guilty of using excessive force.

Blacks in America expected as much, whether in the Mississippi of the 1960s and early '70s or in the California of the '90s. But this time our expectation for justice had been raised. The beating was captured on videotape. Now the whole world could see that blacks were not just making up these cries of police brutality. Surely justice would follow.

When it did not, the anger and frustration of the black community reached a flashpoint. The Rodney King beating had lit the fuse, but the acquittal of the white policemen set off the explosion. And once the fire was started, there was no putting it out.

Was it a one-time blaze?

No, it was not.

The truth is that our country is deeply divided along racial lines. Racial tensions and hatreds smolder barely beneath the surface, needing only a spark—like the Rodney King verdict—to set off the explosion. Explosions are likely in other cities, too, with damage equal to or even greater than what occurred in Los Angeles during the spring of 1992.

Unless things change. Unless we individual Christians, and the Church as a whole, begin investing ourselves to end racism once and for all, to establish justice, to bring about reconciliation.

This is no time to fiddle while America burns, to continue with business as usual while racial hatred and distrust reach the boiling point. This is a time for action. This is a time to begin a journey toward justice. This is a time for the men and women of God to work through Him to bring a miracle of healing and recovery to our divided land.

To Be Young, American . . . and Black

John Perkins

This is the greatest country in the world.

Never before in the history of mankind has there been a nation that has given her people so much in terms of freedom, possibilities and opportunities. It is a thrill to be an American.

Unless you happen to be black.

America, you see, has always been a different place for those who have black skin. We are expected to know our place. We are supposed to be content with our lot and not expect a whole lot more out of life. We are supposed to get by on less than our fellow Americans who happen to be white.

That is the way it has been for most black folks in this country for the last three hundred-plus years, and changes are slow in coming—very slow.

Does it sound like I am bitter? I am not. Does it sound like I am exaggerating? I am not doing that either. All I am doing is telling the truth—a truth every black American knows from personal experience.

If you take issue with what I have said, there can be only one reason: You are white—which means you have most likely been spared a lot of things that are common to blacks.

Please believe me when I say I am not trying to make you angry, nor am I trying to point my finger at you and accuse you of something you did not do. But I do want to open your eyes to the way things are for far too many people here in the United States.

I am talking about people in New York. In California. In Texas. In Illinois. In Mississippi.

Yes, in Mississippi.

That is where I was born in 1930. It did not take me long to figure out I was a second-class citizen. Long before I was old enough to understand what a word like racism meant, I ran into the reality of it on the streets of my hometown.

If we were in town on a Saturday, for example, and we wanted a hamburger or hot dog, we could not just march up to the window and order one. We had to go through the alley to the back door, where we would practically have to beg before we could get anyone to notice us.

The white kids went to school in nice buildings where they had comfortable desks to sit in, well-trained teachers and brand-new textbooks. We went to school in run-down buildings with hand-me-down desks and textbooks and where, all too often, we had teachers who did not know much more about things than we did!

Then there were the school buses.

White kids got to ride to school in big, bright, shiny school buses. Sometimes those buses drove right up to their houses and picked them up. But that was not the way it was for us.

We had to walk to school. It did not matter how far away we lived—three miles, five miles. It did not matter if it was raining or snowing. If we were going to get to school, we had to walk. There was no other way to get there. It was hard sometimes, walking along, tired and cold, to see those white kids zip past us in their shiny yellow buses. It did not make them happy just to think they were riding to school while we had to walk. No, sir. They had to rub it in by bombarding us with spitwads from the windows of their bus, by making faces at us and sticking their tongues out.

And, of course, by calling us names. There were lots of names—but the one I remember most is that universal favorite: "Nigger!"

You know, *nigger* is a word that has always been used in the South. Some white folks use it without a hint of anger or malice in their voices. Black folks are niggers, pure and simple, just as native Americans are Indians. But there is a time when the word *nigger* is used to tell men and women of color exactly who and what they are. The white person's lip curls into a sneer, his nostrils flare and he spits out the word as if it is the worst thing one human being could possibly call another: "Nigger!"

I do not mind telling you that I am proud to be a black American. But I never have been and never will be a nigger. I have never known a nigger. I have never even *met* a nigger. And if I could have my way, I would see to it that a curse was placed on that word so that nobody could ever use it again!

But I have strayed from my subject—which is telling you what it was like to be a black child growing up in the Mississippi of the 1930s and '40s.

Those were difficult and dangerous days. Coming out of the Depression, jobs were scarce, and no white man wanted to risk losing his job to a black man. That is one reason, I think, why poor whites have always been more racist—or at least more openly racist—than middle-class whites. The poor white wants to feel better than *somebody*. He wants to have a better job than somebody. Live in a better house than somebody. Drive a better car than somebody. And in the South—especially the South of the 1930s—the only people he could possibly look down on were those with black faces and hands.

So, as I said, that was a particularly terrible time for us in the southern United States. The Ku Klux Klan was having a heyday keeping us in line. Beatings and lynchings were not uncommon. And it did not take much to anger the Klan.

If you were black, and a white person spoke to you, you had better answer back respectfully, and that meant saying, "Yes, sir" and "No, sir," "Yes, ma'am" and "No, ma'am." It did not matter if you were 70 years old and an 11-year-old child asked you a question. You still had to say, "Yes, sir" or "No, sir," just as if you were talking to a U.S. senator. To show disrespect to a white person in any way was almost akin to committing blasphemy or treason.

Sometimes the Klan, or Klan sympathizers, would beat or even kill someone just for the heck of it. I still do not know why. I suppose it was just to let us know that they were there, they were watching, and we had better toe the line.

I will never forget the time during my adolescence that a group of Klansmen decided, for no apparent reason, to "teach a lesson" to a friend of mine. I went to school with him, and we could not have been any more than 14 or 15 years old when it happened.

He was walking along the road to town, minding his own business, not causing a bit of trouble for anyone, when a carload of Klansmen spotted him. They liked their odds—six to one—and decided they wanted to "have some fun" with this nigger.

Their idea of having some fun was to jump him and beat him nearly half to death. But that was not enough. So while several of them held him down, one of the attackers got out his hunting knife and castrated him, while my friend screamed. Then they flung him into a ditch and went on their way.

Somehow the mutilated boy survived. Some people passing by saw him lying in the ditch, picked him up and took him to a hospital. But by then there was not much the doctors could do for him. He lived but he never recovered. He spent a couple of years lying in bed, and he has been paralyzed ever since.

Now I said that the attack was carried out by the Klan, and that may not be the exact truth. After all, nobody was ever charged with the crime, so it is impossible to say with certainty who did it. All I know is, unprovoked attacks of this type were not uncommon during those days, and if the people who carried them out were not actually members of the Klan, they were certainly following through on the spirit and style of the organization.

There was no arrest, of course, if an attack was carried out by a white person on a black person. Let it be the other way around, though, and an execution was sure to follow—either "legally" or at the hands of a lynch mob. That was just the way it was in the South of my youth.

My childhood was difficult, too, because my mama died when I was only seven months old. My daddy, overcome by his grief, abandoned me soon after that. But the primary reason my childhood was hard was, pure and simple, the color of my skin. Etched forever in my mind are two incidents that drove that point home to me (as if it needed driving home). One was a great and terrible tragedy. The other was almost insignificant in comparison, but for me a tragedy just the same.

The first incident was the murder of my brother Clyde by a white police officer.

I have told the story of Clyde's death before, but it does not get any easier with the telling. And what magnifies the pain for me is the realization that my brother's killing has been repeated many times. There have been hundreds, perhaps even thousands of other "Clydes" in this country—men who have met with the same senseless brutality.

My brother died on a summer's evening in 1946, an oppressively hot day in New Hebron, Mississippi—the kind of day that saps the strength from everyone and causes tempers to flare. Maybe the heat of the day contributed to what happened, but it was no excuse.

My brother had served his country during World War II. He had been right in the thick of the fighting in Germany, where he was wounded. He had come back home with several combat ribbons and a Purple Heart.

That made him a hero to some of us. But not to the white folks in New Hebron. To them he was still just Clyde, and Clyde was, after all was said and done, a nigger. And some of the white folks did not like it that Clyde held his head up a bit higher than he was supposed to, that he looked them in the eye when he talked to them, that he did not shuffle and grin and say, "Yes, sir" or "No, sir" to people half his age.

On this summer afternoon, Clyde and his girlfriend, Emma, were in line waiting to see a movie at Carolyn's Theater in downtown New Hebron. We were not allowed to enter the theater through the front door, of course. We had to stand in line in a narrow alley that ran between the theater and the dime store next door, and buy our tickets at a box office set up at a side entrance that led upstairs to the balcony. It was whites-only territory downstairs.

I was a few blocks away at my friend Charlie's house, but from what I understand, the alley was getting crowded and people were getting impatient because the box office had not yet opened. Apparently there was some pushing and shoving in the crowd—nothing malicious, just some jostling brought on by the heat, the crowded conditions and impatience. A white deputy marshal was there to keep things under control.

"You niggers quiet down!" he shouted. He seemed to be speaking directly to Clyde.

Clyde's attention had been on his girlfriend, but now he turned around to face the deputy. Maybe he wanted to protest that he was not doing anything wrong. Maybe he wanted to ask the deputy if he knew when someone was going to open the box office. Whatever it was he wanted, the deputy decided that Clyde's posture represented a defiance of his authority, and he knew how to deal with defiance. He smacked Clyde a good one with his nightstick right across the side of his head.

Clyde put up his hands, as any man would, to defend himself.

The deputy apparently saw that as another sign of defiance and went to give Clyde another crack. But Clyde was not going to stand there and let the man beat him half to death, so he grabbed the nightstick in self-defense.

That was all the excuse the "law" needed. The deputy pulled his gun from its holster, took two steps back and fired two bullets into Clyde's stomach from almost point-blank range. Then he walked away. As far as he was concerned, Clyde could bleed to death right there in the alley.

Clyde did not die right away. A group picked him up and carried him across the street to the doctor's office. Naturally they had to take him in the back entrance.

A few blocks away, at Charlie's house, I remember a car squealing up and somebody shouting that Clyde had been shot. I thought at first I was hearing it wrong. Surely they could not be talking about my big brother, my hero! It could not be Clyde Perkins they were talking about.

I got to Dr. Langston's office as soon as I could, and when I saw my brother, my heart shriveled up within me. I think I knew right away he was not going to make it, but I could not let myself believe it. His breathing was labored and his eyes were dull, almost as if they were already beginning to lose the light.

"Please, brother," I begged him, "don't die!"

Bitter and angry tears burned my eyes, but I would not let them fall. The deputy who had shot my brother was in that doctor's office, too, looking on from a distance, cold and dispassionate, "keeping things under control." I would not let myself cry in front of that man. I hated him too much to let him see me cry.

I also knew at that instant that if I had had a gun, I would have shot that man. If I had had a gun with twenty bullets in it, I would have shot him twenty times. I can only thank God now that I did *not* have a gun.

I stroked Clyde's cheek as Dr. Langston worked on him. The doctor, who was white, seemed to be trying hard to save Clyde's life, but also looked moment by moment as if he was not going to win this battle.

Finally Dr. Langston shook his head.

"I've done all I can," he announced. The way he said it let us know immediately that he knew it was not enough. "You have to get him to the hospital."

Getting him to the hospital was not easy. It meant taking him all the way to Jackson, the state capital, which was nearly ninety minutes away, partly over rough gravel roads.

Still, we had to try.

We eased Clyde into the back seat of a '41 Chevy belonging to my cousin, Joe David. I got in the back, too, with Clyde's head in my lap, and asked God to please give my brother a miracle. But there was to be no miracle that hot summer night.

We drove like mad all the way to Jackson, yet I have never been in a car that seemed to move so slowly. I cannot remember another ninety minutes that might as well have been ninety hours or even ninety days. The road to Jackson seemed to go on forever . . . and Clyde seemed to die a little more with each mile. By the time we reached Jackson, he was barely hanging onto life.

If you have ever sat in an emergency room waiting room, praying with all your being that the doctor will walk through that door and give you some good news, then you have some idea of what the next few hours were like. Some people put Clyde on a stretcher and carried him into the hospital. I remember being in a room with him—I suppose it was Intensive Care, but I am not really sure. A lot of other people were in there, and I sat observing it all, but I was too numb to absorb anything. It was happening all around me, but I was not really a part of it.

Until the doctor came through that door. His news was not good.

My brother was dead.

My brother, who had put his life on the line God knows how many times fighting to keep this country free. My brother, who had wanted to prove to me that a black kid growing up on the wrong side of town in New Hebron, Mississippi, could amount to something. He was dead, for no good reason at all.

I took Clyde's death hard. You do not just get over something like that. Back then, there was not even an investigation to determine whether the deputy marshal had used excessive force. There was no need for an investigation because Clyde was black, the man who shot him was white, and in the eyes of the power structure, that settled it.

I still take Clyde's death hard, even though it happened nearly fifty years ago. Sometimes I think about who he could have been and what he could have contributed to society. This world will never know how much it missed, simply because a white man with a badge was not going to let some "uppity nigger" sass or challenge him.

There is not a single doubt in my mind that Clyde was shot and killed for no reason other than that he was black. There is no way in the world that any deputy would have used his weapon on a young white man who was making too much noise while waiting in line to see a movie.

Black lives just did not count for much in Mississippi in those days. I had seen the truth of that statement many times by my sixteenth birthday, but it was the murder of my brother Clyde that made it a personal reality to me.

The second tragedy that helped open my eyes to the reality of racism was much smaller, but it still had a profound effect on the way I looked at life. Its lesson was the same: "You're not worth as much as a white person."

I do not want you to get the wrong idea and think I accepted that line of reasoning—that I thought I *was* inferior because I was black. Not even for an instant did I think that way. I knew I was just as good as anybody else, no matter what anybody thought. At the same time I knew that most of the whites in New Hebron were looking down their noses at me—and I suppose I figured it would have been that way anywhere else in the world, too.

Anyway, I was twelve when I hired myself out to a white man who was in a hurry to get several tons of hay into his barns. It looked like rainy weather was headed our way, and he knew that if he did not get all that hay inside, it might be ruined.

It never occurred to me to set my price beforehand. I simply told the man I would help him, figuring that if I put in a good day's work, he would have to pay me at least a dollar and a half, maybe even two dollars. This was the going rate and I knew it.

Let me tell you, I never worked so hard in my life. By the end of the day I had begun to think that even two dollars was not going to be enough! Then again, I wanted to do the very best job I could so the man might hire me again sometime. After all, a boy of twelve can always use some extra spending money.

Well, at the end of that day, that man seemed to appreciate all my hard work. He told me so. Then he went to get the money he owed me.

"This is for you!" he said with a tone that made it sound as if he were dropping the crown jewels into my hand.

When I looked into my palm, what I saw was a far cry from diamonds and rubies. It was fifteen cents! Fifteen lousy cents for a full day's work.

I was too shocked to say anything. So I just stood there staring at that dime and buffalo nickel, wishing I had not worked quite so hard. As the shock began to wear off, a flash of anger shot through me. I wanted to take that money and throw it back in his face. But I was afraid to show the least little bit of displeasure. After all, I was black, he was white, and I knew even at twelve that it was not very smart to make waves. Neither was it very smart to appear to be unappreciative.

"What's the matter, boy? Cat got your tongue?"

"Uh . . . no, sir. Thank you, sir."

I put the fifteen cents in my pocket and walked out of that man's house and I never went back.

But as I walked away, I felt anger surging through me once again. This time it was not so much that the man had cheated me. I was angry because he thought I should be happy with fifteen cents. He thought I was so dumb that I would think fifteen cents was a fair price for a hard day's work.

And why would he think a thing like that? Pure and simple, because I was black.

I could tell you at least a dozen other incidents that happened to me when I was a young man. I won't because I have already made my point. But I will say this: Not a black person in this country has not been touched by racism in some way. My experiences as a child have been repeated time and again in the lives of millions of children everywhere in the United States.

One more thing about the state where I grew up. I have no facts to back me up on this, but I would not be surprised to find out that Mississippi has more Christian churches per capita than any other state. Let me take that a step further. It would not surprise me to find out that Mississippi is the "church capital" of the world. Mississippi is right in the heart of what they call the Bible Belt, and by and large Mississippians are Bible-believing, churchgoing people.

But you know what? Not once when I was a child did I ever hear a leader from one of Mississippi's white churches speak out against racism. Never did I hear *any* white Christian say, "Brothers, what we've been doing is wrong! We've got to realize that *all* people are created in the image of God—blacks, too—and we've got to start treating them as our equals."

As a matter of fact, just the reverse was true. The white churches of Mississippi were for the most part defenders of the status quo, preaching segregation from the pulpit as God's perfect plan for the races.

Those days may be gone. But the fruit they produced remains. And Sunday morning is still the most segregated day of the week.

Brothers and sisters, we have to change that. And we must do it now, before it is too late.

How I Learned to Hate

3

Tom Tarrants

"Two, four, six, eight! We don't want to integrate!"

That was the belligerent cry that echoed across the grounds of Murphy High School. Murphy was the leading high school in the city and had a proud tradition. My parents had attended there before me.

But today dozens of National Guard troops surrounded the sprawling campus, along with uniformed policemen and U.S. marshals.

No one liked what was going on here.

The year was 1963. The place was Mobile, Alabama. The impetus for this angry gathering: the enrollment of two new black students in our school. Our school had been ordered by the federal government to integrate, and federal marshals had escorted two black girls that morning into the building.

The reaction of the two thousand white students was virtually unanimous. We did not want those blacks in our school. A smaller group was prepared to protest. So they gathered in front of the school's main entrance—shouting, screaming, ready and willing to do whatever it took to keep those black girls out of our school.

I was among them.

The battle at Murphy High School was the first of my many encounters with the law over the next few years. As a result of my involvement, I was suspended from school for a couple of weeks. But I didn't care. I had decided that there was something much more important than school: doing everything within my power to save America from the Jews and blacks who threatened to bring her down.

I grew up in a fairly normal Southern middle-class home.

My father worked in the automobile business, sometimes in management, more often in sales. Mother stayed home and took care of me and my younger sister and brother. We often saw aunts, uncles and grandparents, most of whom lived within a few miles of us in Mobile. Until junior high, I was a pretty good student and led a more or less normal life. But around this time things began to deteriorate.

I am sure that Mobile, Alabama, in the early 1960s was pretty much like everywhere else in the United States. People were interested in Elvis Presley or the Beatles, fast cars, our favorite football teams, and whether the Russians were going to beat us to the moon.

I was a pretty typical boy. I had some friends and got good enough grades—at least until junior high. I was a show-off and cut-up at times, but I was not particularly angry, did not get into many fights and was certainly not consciously a racist. In fact, my family had a black maid, Mary, whom everyone thought was wonderful, including me. We loved her almost like a member of the family.

I do not think I ever heard either of my parents say anything ugly about black people. They supported segregation, of course, when the integration crisis came, but so did everyone else in the South in those days. Segregation was the only world we knew. We didn't question it; it was the way things had always been. Furthermore, everyone pretty much figured it was the way black people wanted it to be, too. We all knew they would rather stay with their own kind. They wanted to live on their own side of town, eat in their own restaurants, go to their own movies, attend their own sporting events.

When you are born into a social/cultural system in which everyone around you thinks and behaves as you do, you are not likely
to question your value system. I did not question mine. Segregation was right because it had always been that way, and everyone
knew it should stay that way because blacks were not equal to
whites.

There were plenty of black people in Mobile. I even knew some
of them by name. Until desegregation I treated them with respect.
At least I thought I did. But I did not want them as my next-door
neighbors or best friends, and I certainly did not want to go to
school with them. White was white, and black was black, and
never the twain should mix.

Then the federal government stepped in and forever changed
the face of the American South. It was a change that did not come
easily, or quickly, or without resistance, or without a great deal of
pain for millions of people, black and white alike. For me personally, this change set into motion a chain of cataclysmic reactions. Before it was all over, I would become a hardened, hate-
filled terrorist, very nearly lose my life in two bloody gun battles
with police and FBI agents, see two friends die before my eyes,
critically wound a policeman and be the sole resident of a six-by-
nine-foot cell in the maximum security unit of the Mississippi State
Prison.

All this began in 1963 with the admission of those two black
students into Murphy High School.

Looking back on it now, I can only admire those two girls for
their courage in walking into the hostile environment of Murphy
that day. Maybe they did not want to be there. Maybe they were
willing to break the color barrier at our high school only at their
parents' insistence.

I never knew why they were at Murphy because I never asked
them. I did not care why they were there. All I knew was, they had
no business being there. They were an unwelcome presence and
an affront to the way things were supposed to be. If they had not
been accompanied by armed federal marshals and the National
Guard, they would have been in real danger. There was an irra-

tional anger and hatred toward them in that high school that could have cost them dearly.

I doubt there is anything as ugly and dangerous as self-righteous anger, which is what had us in its grip. None of us doubted that we were right and they were wrong, and being right gave us a license to do just about anything to get our way.

Things settled down somewhat after our initial violent protest, but life could not have been easy for those girls. They took quite a bit of verbal abuse. They were ridiculed in class and jostled in the hallways. Because nobody wanted them there, students and teachers alike, we did not hesitate to make that crystal clear. I took every opportunity I got to call them niggers.

As far as I know, there was never any real trouble involving either one of them. They managed to hang in there somehow, weather the storm and pave the way for the thousands of other black students who have attended Murphy High since then.

But as upsetting as the presence of those black students was, even worse for most of us was the fact that the federal government was telling us what to do. This was a gross violation of states' rights. It was *our* business whether we wanted to have black students in our schools. And since we clearly did not, nobody should have the right to make us take them in. We might as well have been under attack by Union soldiers. General Sherman marching to the sea and burning everything in his path could not have stirred up more anger than was felt by many, if not most, of the white residents of Mobile.

The spirit of rebellion and anger at Murphy High School, and in the region in general, was both contagious and exhilarating. Not even high school football had ever brought people together the way the forced integration of our schools did. Nothing brings people together faster than a common enemy. And we had a common enemy, an enemy reflected in the often sad, sometimes frightened but always determined faces of two black teenagers who simply wanted the right to a good education.

The enemy itself, I realized, was the officials in Washington, and particularly in the Justice Department, who were out to ruin our way of life. Those pointy-headed liberals did not understand us.

They did not even *try* to know how we felt, but seemed determined to step on us, grind us into the ground and take away our freedom. They seemed hell-bent on undermining America and everything she stood for, beginning with the South.

It did not help my outlook that I was going through quite a bit of adolescent rebellion and inner turbulence at the time. My parents' marriage was shaky, and words like *separation* and *divorce* kept finding their way into the conversation. Also, probably due in large part to what was happening between my parents, I found myself feeling more estranged from my father. I was angry that he drank too much, that he was not nicer to my mother, that he did not try harder to get along with her. But then, it did not seem to me that he tried very hard to be nice to me, either. I am sure that part of my anger toward those who were forcing the integration of our schools was, in reality, repressed anger toward my father.

But due to the turmoil of those times, what appeared to be the impending breakup of my parents' marriage was even harder to take than it might otherwise have been. It seemed to me that my family was disintegrating at the same time the world was falling apart—my comfortable, well-defined world in which everybody knew his place and acted accordingly, where whites were superior and blacks were inferior and stayed in their place.

Like most sixteen-year-olds, I was not sure who I was, what my purpose was or what I would do with my life. I needed something to believe in, a cause to which I could dedicate myself.

Early in 1963, before the integration of Murphy High School, I had decided that I would get involved in helping change the political system. I had jumped into the Draft Goldwater Campaign that was just getting underway. As far as I was concerned, it was more than a campaign; it was a crusade. Barry Goldwater absolutely *had* to win that election.

It was not hard to work for Barry Goldwater in Alabama, not exactly sticking your neck out on behalf of an unpopular cause. Alabama had long been a Democratic stronghold, but many of her people were disgusted with Kennedy and Johnson over the race issue and were open to Goldwater's conservative politics. When the 1964 election came, in fact, Lyndon Johnson, who had succeeded Kennedy, did not even appear on the ballot in Alabama, Georgia, Louisiana, Mississippi and South Carolina. Barry Goldwater won each of these states by a landslide.

But they were just about all he won, as Lyndon Johnson rolled to victory in what was, up until that time, one of the most one-sided wins ever in a U.S. presidential election. I remember the night the election returns came in. I sat in front of the television dumbfounded by the vote tallies being reported. It could not be true! It was horrible to think that the United States was going right down the drain and nobody seemed to realize it or to care. I did not feel good, or smug, wrapped in the knowledge that I knew something most people did not know. I wanted to warn them, get them to wake up. But how? What could I do?

Barry Goldwater, I thought, was a great American, not least because he understood the importance of states' rights.

States' rights had been the rallying cry of the old Dixiecrats since the 1940s. The Dixiecrats felt that the federal government had no right to tell individual states what to do. It was O.K. to have a partnership with Washington when it came to building roads or financing big public works projects . . . but when it came to their laws and courts, that was where states did not need any interference from the federal government.

In other words, states' rights meant that if the state of Alabama did not think any black students should attend Murphy High School in Mobile, then that's the way it would be.

Barry Goldwater believed in individual freedom. He did not think it was fair to pass things like fair housing laws. If a person owned rental property, he should have the right to rent or not rent that property to whomever he chose. The federal government had no right interfering in such matters. Goldwater had said that "extremism in defense of liberty is no vice," and that is exactly how I felt. Sometimes extreme measures were needed. This was such a time and I was ready to take them.

The things Goldwater said sounded pretty good to the beleaguered white residents of Alabama, and we hoped a Goldwater administration would undo most of the civil rights damage Kennedy and Johnson had inflicted on us.

I am not really sure when it happened, but it was not long before I concluded that Goldwater's victory would not be enough to solve our problems. This thought took firm root in my mind as a result of meeting some people in the Draft Goldwater Campaign who belonged to the John Birch Society. Through attending their meetings and reading their literature, I became convinced that our nation was in far deeper trouble than I had first thought. An international Communist conspiracy had long ago penetrated the highest levels of our government, especially the State Department, and was undermining us from within.

If I had any doubt about the reality and danger of the Communist threat, it was dispelled when I read J. Edgar Hoover's *Masters of Deceit* in the school library. Even the director of the FBI confirmed it. And if you cannot work within the system, you have to work outside of it! As my thinking moved along these lines, I soon concluded that working within the system was hopeless, and that I would *have* to work outside of it.

This thought was strengthened by my conversations with Robert M. Smith, one of the men I met soon after the protest at Murphy High School.

Smith, who was director in Mobile of J. B. Stoner's National States' Rights Party, was older and more experienced than I. He, too, hated LBJ, but he did not like Goldwater. Goldwater was a Jew, and Smith was not fond of any Jew.

Smith seemed to like me, and I spent as much time as I could visiting with him in his Mobile office. He let me know right away that there was more at stake here than even I realized. He seemed to know a lot about sinister goings-on, and I longed to gain entrance into the inner circle where men like Smith knew what was really happening in our country.

Through his influence, I became deeply involved in the local chapter of the National States' Rights Party. J.B. Stoner, who had been active in Georgia politics for years, made no bones about how he felt. To Stoner, blacks were niggers and Jews were hebes or kikes. These and similar terms filled the numerous speeches he gave throughout the South, and they also filled the pages of *The Thunderbolt*, a newspaper I read avidly. I was becoming a true believer and began to read everything I could find that would support my increasingly radical thinking.

(Many thousands continue to believe. Stoner is dead now, but *The Thunderbolt* is still in business. Its message of unreasoning hatred aimed at an entire race of people continues to find a wide audience.)

About this time I also came in contact with the teachings of Wesley Swift and his Church of Jesus Christ—Christian, forerunner of the Aryan Nation movement. Through Swift's teaching, I learned the amazing truth that Jesus Christ was not a Jew but a blue-eyed, blond-haired, light-skinned Aryan. The notion that Jesus had been Semitic was just another Jewish perversion of history.

Swift spread his teaching through his church, a newspaper, a variety of other publications and taped sermons. The church had altars covered with swastikas and pictures of Adolf Hitler on the walls. Members of Swift's church wore black armbands and gave each other the Nazi salute—all in the name of Christianity.

The fact that it was easy for me to believe everything Swift taught illustrates how far gone I was. I would have believed anything that gave me a reason for the hatred I felt or that made me feel more strongly about the importance of my involvement in "the cause."

Another man I met at this time was John Crommelin, a retired Navy admiral. "The Admiral," as we called him, hosted me on several visits to his country estate near Montgomery, where we talked for hours about the threats facing our country, not just from the civil rights movement but from the international Jewish conspiracy.

I do not remember who was responsible for publishing the literature he gave me to read, but I do remember its urgent tone, its prophetic voice and its call to action. The gist of it was that America was in real trouble—especially white America. All over the world, it explained, conspirators had been working out a sinister plan that threatened to doom us all. This conspiracy involved the weakening of white America through the "mongrelization" of the races. Naturally, the civil rights movement was one of the ways this was being done.

I did not question any of what I read. I had heard it before. It was horrible to think it might be true, but it was also exciting, because it meant that the battle in which I was getting involved was even more important than I had suspected. This went beyond the right of an individual state to write and enforce its own laws. The very future of the United States of America was at stake. The survival of the Christian white race depended on people like me doing everything we could to thwart the conspirators.

That last point is important, because the material I was given to read claimed to be Christian in its outlook. Looking back on it now, I know that its message was very distorted, even demonic. It claimed that the conspirators were a godless and evil bunch who would like nothing better than to bring Christian America to its knees, lock the doors to all of our churches and force us at gunpoint to deny Jesus.

It was dramatic, but I took it very seriously. I wanted to read more. And there was much more to read.

I read everything I could get my hands on and more besides. It all rang true because it reinforced my prejudices.

The belief at the core of all this ideology was that the Jews are out to dominate the world. They have accumulated great power and influence through their wealth and political connections. Their international banking houses influence world events, have financed revolutions and even hold entire nations captive to their whims.

This propaganda, lumping all Jews together, "proved" that it was the Jews who were responsible for the Bolshevik Revolution in Russia in 1917. In fact, Karl Marx had been a Jew, the grandson of a rabbi. From this it inferred that Communism itself was actually a Jewish plot—one of the ways by which this evil race of people was out to dominate the world.

There were many facets to this Jewish plot for world control. It was said, for example, that Jews owned all the major media and publishing companies, since many of their presidents were Jewish. (I did not know enough about business at that time to realize that nearly all major corporations are owned by stockholders—thousands of them, Jew and Gentile, liberal and conservative.) It was also purported that you could not trust what you saw on the news because that was controlled by the Jews. Chances were you could not trust the books you read, because they were slanted to present the Jewish point of view. We even doubted that the Holocaust took place, insisting instead that the Jews had revised history to further their own purposes. Some writers went so far as to insist that the millions of people who had been exterminated during the 1930s and '40s were "decent German citizens" who had starved to death because of the greed and selfishness of the Jews, who controlled that country's means of production and wealth.

Author James Burnham in his book *Suicide of the West* gives a brilliant description of our ideological thinking:

> A convinced believer in the anti-semitic ideology tells me that the Bolshevik Revolution is a Jewish plot. I point out to him that the revolution was led to its first major victory by a non-Jew, Lenin. He then explains that Lenin was the pawn of Trotsky, Radek, Kamenev and Zinoviev, and other Jews who were in the Bolshevik High Command. I remind him that Lenin's successor as leader of the revolution, the non-Jew Stalin, killed off all those Jews; and that Stalin has been followed by the non-Jew Khrushchev, under whose rule there have been notable revivals of anti-semitic attitudes and conduct. He then informs me that the seeming Soviet anti-semitism is only a fraud invented by the Jewish press, and that Stalin and Khrushchev are really Jews whose names have been changed with a total substitution of forged records.
>
> Suppose I am able to present documents that even he will have to admit show this to be impossible. He is still unmoved. He tells me that the real Jewish center that controls the revolution and the entire world conspiracy is not in Russia anyway, but in Antwerp, Tel Aviv, Lhasa, New York, or somewhere, and that it has deliberately eliminated the Jews from the public officialdom of the Bolshevik countries in order to conceal its hand and deceive the world about what is going on.

The material I was reading asserted that the civil rights movement was one of the ways the Jewish conspirators were trying to gain control over the United States. If they could bring about a mixing of the races, a pollution of the superior white race, it would lower our intelligence, weaken our cultural vigor and enable us to be dominated more easily.

It naturally followed that even though we hated the blacks for their intrusion into our world, our real hatred was reserved for the Jews. It was the Jews who were really responsible for what was going on. The blacks were only pawns in the Jews' evil game. We knew, after all, that the civil rights movement was loaded with Communists and Communist sympathizers. And, as I mentioned earlier, Communism was really nothing more than a Jewish fraternity.

The deeper I got into this insidious propaganda and "ideological thinking," the more isolated I became from reality. It would be accurate to say, in fact, that we developed an alternate reality— or, rather, unreality. Before long the only friends I had were those as deeply immersed in this thinking as I was. Nobody I knew questioned any of it, nor did I. We reinforced each other in our beliefs, in our hatred and in our willingness to put our lives on the line in defense of Christianity, freedom and the white race.

Those of us who shared this secret knowledge felt a special bond of camaraderie fostered by the fact that we had insights that the world in general did not have. It was this that made the Ku Klux Klan, with its mysticism, secrecy and oaths, so appealing. By the time I was 20, my involvement in the Klan was the most important thing in my life.

I was not alone in my delusions. Thousands of others believed the same things—and still do. In fact, the climate in this country now is right for the Klan to grow and conspiracy theories to flourish again.

The more I read and heard, the more angry and alarmed I became about what was going on. Clearly the conspirators were winning, and they *had* to be stopped. Whatever it took to stop them, I was willing to do. I surrounded myself more and more with people who felt the same way.

A few of us in Mobile founded an organization called the Christian Military Defense League, and we set out to defend our faith with such Christian acts as making threatening phone calls to rabbis and black leaders, letting them know we were watching them and warning them to tone things down if they wanted to stay out of trouble. We also struck some defiant blows against the conspiracy through such activities as painting swastikas on synagogue walls. We talked about taking stronger measures, but we never got any farther than talk.

After a while I was embarrassed and frustrated by what I considered to be our small and insignificant acts in the face of a massive, worldwide conspiracy that threatened the entire free world. Stronger measures were clearly called for, and I intended to respond accordingly. I was not going to let the conspirators win without a fight. Sooner or later it was all going to come down to a race war, and when it did, I intended to be ready.

The U.S. Constitution gave me the right to bear arms, and I intended to bear as many of them as I could. I bought several guns and thousands of rounds of ammunition. I spent hour after hour on the range sharpening my marksmanship. No matter how many guns I had, though, it was not enough. Pistols, rifles, shotguns, even submachine guns—I had them all. Large caliber, small caliber and everything in between. I hoarded guns and ammunition, and so did my friends. I also began to read everything I could find on the CIA and KGB and on guerrilla warfare and the use of explosive devices.

At one point during this period I decided that I would join the Army Rangers or Special Forces so I could fight the Communists in Vietnam—but at the very last minute I changed my mind. Why? Because the Vietnam war was Lyndon Johnson's war, and I hated Lyndon Johnson.

But now I was prepared to become a guerrilla fighter. I knew beyond any doubt that I was willing to fight for what I believed in, and I was not willing to wait patiently for the battle to come to me. Instead, I would take the initiative and choose the time and place of engagement on terms favorable to me.

This mentality soon found expression. In the small Alabama town of Prichard, I provoked a fight one day with a black man who ran a service station. I would probably have killed him in "self-defense," but the police arrested me before I could do it. They confiscated my automatic shotgun in the process but let me off with a warning.

A few weeks later, States' Rights Party leader Bob Smith and I were stopped by police while we were driving through a black neighborhood in Mobile. Once again I was looking for a fight. Once again I was armed—and the Mobile police were not willing to let me off so lightly. I was arrested and charged with possessing an illegal weapon, a sawed-off shotgun. This time I had to go to federal court because the gun violated federal law. But the judge, hoping I had learned a lesson, placed me on probation, letting me off with a few harsh words. He warned me that I had been keeping "bad company," and he said, "If I ever hear of you with a gun again—even a shotgun going dove hunting—I will revoke your probation."

"Yes, sir," I said at my polite Southern best.

But I knew, before I had even walked out of that courtroom, that my role in the war was just beginning. I was no common criminal. I was fighting in a battle for the future of our country.

Sometime later I learned about a man named Sam Bowers who was the head of the White Knights of the Ku Klux Klan. I admired Bowers, because his organization had proven that it was willing to do more than talk. Bowers and seventeen other members of the White Knights were about to go on trial for the murders in Mississippi of three civil rights workers from Philadelphia.

The disappearance of those three young men—two white and one black—and the subsequent discovery of their bodies beneath an earthen dam had made major news headlines all across the United States. I was so full of hatred by this time that my friends and I rejoiced when the bodies of those young men were found. We figured they had gotten what they deserved, and we talked about doing the same thing to a few more of those "agitators" who had come into our state. If Bowers was involved in the killing of those three young men, he was my kind of man.

Bowers had also been indicted in the murder of NAACP leader Vernon Dahmer—so far as I was concerned, another feather in his cap.

I wanted to work with him. I thought he was a great man. Just imagine what I could do teamed up with a man like that!

Part

Hearts Aflame

Into the Fire 4

John Perkins

I never thought I would go back to Mississippi—at least not to stay. It might be all right to visit occasionally—to see my family and some of our old friends. But as far as a place to live, I was happy to leave Mississippi behind.

A lot of things happened to me after my brother Clyde was killed. One of those things was a trip to California to stay with my cousin. My uncle and aunt sent me out West so I would not meet the same fate as my brother.

It did not take me long to decide that this was more than a visit. I was going to leave Mississippi, and all that it represented, far behind me. I loved California, and not just because of the weather or the beaches. In California it did not seem to matter what color your skin was. I ran into a racist comment or act every now and then, of course, but compared to the way things were in Mississippi, California was paradise.

For another thing, jobs were plentiful there, and they were open to anyone willing to work hard. My first job, at the Union Pacific Foundry, paid me the princely sum of 98 cents an hour. That was not bad money in 1947, and it was a whole lot more than the twenty dollars a month I had been making in New Hebron. I worked right alongside white men, earning the same money they were making, and I could scarcely believe it. What's more, those white men seemed to respect me.

When our company's production increased dramatically due to implementation of newer technology, and the company did not seem inclined to cut us in on increased profits, I helped organize a strike that succeeded in winning us several new benefits.

I knew very well that in New Hebron, Mississippi, nothing like that could ever have happened. There, a black man had to stay in his place or he would be considered uppity and arrogant. In California I felt that my actions were appreciated by my fellow workers and respected by management. That was an unbelievably heady experience.

An even more unbelievable experience happened to me when I went back to New Hebron for a visit during the summer of 1949.

Her name was Vera Mae Young.

It was a Sunday afternoon and I was hanging around on the church grounds of the Pleasant Hill Baptist Church. Believe me when I tell you I was not there to hear anything the preacher had to say. Far from it. I did not have the least interest in Christianity. As far as I was concerned, Christianity was the white man's religion, little more than another way to keep us in line. (Remember that in those days many white churches in the South were preaching segregation and the inferiority of the black race, and there were few if any black churches willing to challenge that kind of thinking.)

No, the reason I was at Pleasant Hill that fine Sunday afternoon was simply because there was nowhere else to go—especially not for a young black man in a small Mississippi town like New Hebron. I was there to shoot the breeze with my friends, and because there was usually some pretty good eating at the potluck after the worship service.

But when I saw Vera Mae walk out of that church building, I forgot about every other reason for being there. All my attention was on her, and I just knew I had to meet that girl. A few years earlier I might have let her walk out of my life without trying to speak to her. But my successes in California had given me confidence.

My eyes followed her as she got into a car with a girlfriend and the two of them sat there talking. Then the rest of me followed her, too. I walked up to the car and talked to her for a few minutes.

I had not been there too long when I said, "I know who would make me a good wife."

I know that won't go down as one of the great opening lines in history, but she didn't laugh.

Instead she smiled and said, "You do? Who?"

"Vera Mae," I said, "you're going to be my wife someday."

After that startling proclamation—what amounted to a proposal, really—we spent some more time talking. But within a couple of days it was time for me to return to California. I did not see her again for two full years, although we kept the post office busy. It soon became apparent that my first assessment of her had been correct. I really did want her to be my wife.

In 1951 I received greetings from Uncle Sam in the form of a draft notice. But before the time came for me to report to the Army, I took another trip to Mississippi to see some of my friends—especially Vera Mae.

I wound up spending most of my time with her. And with every moment that passed, I became more certain that I wanted to spend the rest of my life with her. Suddenly there was an urgency to the matter. So as soon as I finished basic training, I sent for Vera Mae to come to California and we were married. A few weeks later I was shipped overseas and did not see her again for eighteen months—the longest and loneliest eighteen months of my life.

Yet being in the Army was a good experience for me. It broadened my horizons by taking me to places I had scarcely heard of before, and by introducing me to a variety of opinions on political and social issues. Because the Korean War was raging at that time, I did quite a bit of reading on the differences between capitalism and Communism. Soon I was reading almost everything I could find—making as many trips as I could to the troop information centers and libraries. For the first time in my life I was beginning to see the bigger picture of what was going on in the world.

It was at this time that I began to see the black man's struggle against oppression as much more than a personal matter. Growing up in the South, I had always seen it as me against the white man's system. Now I understood that an entire race of people needed to rise up and throw off their chains—and I also saw that there was historical precedent for such a thing to happen.

I learned that there have been all sorts of revolutionary movements in the history of this world. Some have been huge, others have been tiny. Some came with a great deal of noise and excitement, while others passed almost unnoticed until their effects were felt. But the most important thing I learned was that revolution was possible—that people working together could bring about sweeping changes in society.

I do not want to give the wrong impression and make it sound as if I came out of the Army as a revolutionary. Not at all. I was still interested mostly in how I could get ahead in the world. But along with what I had learned organizing the strike at the foundry, the knowledge I gained in the Army gave me the framework I would use years later organizing protest marches and boycotts in Mississippi. I was convinced that our problems were political in nature, and I looked forward to the day when we would rise up and demand to be treated like human beings.

Actually, I should qualify that statement. As far as I was concerned, I looked forward to the day when those of us who lived south of the Mason-Dixon line would rise up and demand to be treated like human beings. Later on I would discover that racism was rampant everywhere in the United States. But at that time I still considered myself fortunate to have been able to "escape" Mississippi, and I figured that when I left the South, I left racism and injustice behind me.

Then something happened that showed me that the real hope for us did not lie in political unity alone, but in the love of Jesus Christ. I discovered that the so-called "white man's religion" was really for everyone—and it was the greatest discovery of my life.

I had known that Vera Mae was a Christian when I met her, which was fine with me. She could be anything she wanted, just as long as she would also be my wife. But I was not interested in her religion, and I let her know right from the start. It was not that I was antagonistic toward her beliefs; I just was not interested in them for myself.

As time went by, my lack of interest began to take its toll on her. She stopped going to church as often. We began to dabble in different religions—a little bit here and a little bit there—looking for something with lasting meaning and value.

Through all our searching and dabbling, Vera Mae attended the worship services occasionally at a Baptist church in Monrovia, where we lived. She liked that church because it had an excellent choir. Sometimes I went with her, and even did some ushering there, but I never paid much attention to the words that were spoken from the pulpit. I suppose my prejudice against Christianity was too strong, back in those days, to ever think that I would find the meaning of life in a small Baptist church.

We were doing pretty well in life at this time. We lived in a nice house, in a good neighborhood, and had plenty of friends. But still, something was missing, and I just could not figure out what it might be.

The answer to my search came from a most unexpected source: our oldest son, Spencer, still a little boy, who had begun attending a children's Bible class at a small church near our house. Spencer was not yet old enough to attend school, but I could see that what he was learning at that Bible study was having a profound effect on him. He was so happy, so peaceful. I was intrigued.

I did not understand at the time that little Spencer had had a personal encounter with Jesus Christ. All I knew was that he loved his Bible class and wanted me to go with him. So I did.

About this time a good friend of mine from work, Calvin Bourne, began putting pressure on me to visit his church—Bethlehem Church of Christ Holiness.

Because I loved my son, and because I wanted to please my friend, I did what they wanted.

What was *really* happening was that the Holy Spirit had begun His irresistible work in my life. I began reading the Bible, and it seemed to speak directly to me. I had always thought of the Bible as nothing more than a musty old book full of superstitious myths. How wrong I had been!

The change in me was finally completed on a Sunday morning in 1957. I do not remember the exact date, but I do remember the

Scripture text for the pastor's sermon: Romans 6:23, "For the wages of sin is death, but the gift of God is eternal life in Christ Jesus our Lord."

Wages were important to me. Not because I was money-hungry, but because they symbolized what a man was worth. My mind went back to that time I received just fifteen cents for a very hard day's work. I thought about the job I had had in Mississippi before I left for the West Coast that paid me twenty dollars a month. And I thought about how proud I had been when my first job in California paid me several times that amount.

What wages would I be paid for the life I was living? I could see that Sunday morning beyond any doubt that I was a sinner, and that death is the only wage to be paid at the end of a life of sin. I also realized for the first time that God had already paid the wages of my sin—that He had sent His Son to die in my place, and all I had to do was accept His free gift. I had never seen myself or my need so clearly. But at long last I knew there was a way of escape.

I almost could not wait until the end of the service so I could surrender my life publicly to Christ.

And when I did, it was the greatest moment I had ever known. Immediately I felt His cleansing love and peace flow through me, and I knew that John Perkins was never going to be the same. I was set free from all my guilt, my frustrations, my sorrows, and I overflowed with love for everyone! It was as if I had been stumbling around in the darkness for the first 27 years of my life, and now somebody had come in, flipped on the switch and flooded my life with light.

I was overwhelmed by the happiness I felt and could not wait to start telling others about Christ so they could experience the same joy. I told everyone I knew—friends, neighbors, co-workers, relatives.

There is an old song that starts out, "I love to tell the story. . . ." That song describes exactly the way it was with me. I loved telling people about what Jesus did on the cross.

I began to conduct child evangelism classes every day. We met in home groups on Sunday afternoon. I went into prison camps to talk to the young men there. I saw many lives changed—not by the power of my testimony, but by the Holy Spirit drawing the lost to Christ. I also knew that God wanted something more from me. He had a specially designed work for me to do. And as the next two years went by, the nature of that work became clearer and clearer.

He was calling me back to Mississippi.

He wanted me to preach the Word to people who thought, as I once had, that Christianity was "a white man's religion." He wanted me to follow Christ, who said that He had been sent

To preach the gospel to the poor
To heal the brokenhearted
To proclaim liberty to the captives
And recovery of sight to the blind
To set at liberty those who are oppressed
To proclaim the acceptable year of the Lord.

(see Luke 4:18–19)

After all, there were few people poorer than the millions of blacks living in Mississippi and other Southern states. Certainly many of them were brokenhearted, due to the conditions in which they lived. Those who discarded Christ because they thought He was a "white man's God" were certainly blind. Were they oppressed? Absolutely. And some of them had been waiting years and years and years hoping that things somehow would get better. I aimed to tell them that now was the time for their lives to change. Today was the day for them to let the power of God's love set them free.

God made it clear to me in many ways that He was calling me back to Mississippi—but one of the most powerful involved a sermon I preached one morning in a prison camp for youthful offenders. These boys were between the ages of 13 and 17. Most of them were black. There were probably thirty or forty of them listening to me that morning, and I poured my heart into my talk.

When it came time for the altar call, only two boys came to surrender their lives to Christ. I knew when I talked to them after the service that, unless God really took hold of them, they were both headed for terrible trouble. I also knew that, were it not for the grace of God, my life could have gone the way theirs had.

They were poor boys with nothing much in the way of an education who were trying to make it in a white man's world. Because they did not feel they could compete on an equal basis with the white man—and due to the circumstances of their lives, they could not—they had turned to crime and wound up in this minimum-security prison camp. The way they were going, the state prison waited just around the corner.

As I talked to those two that morning, I could not help but think about how much God loved them. I knew He cared for them every bit as much as He cared for me—yet my life was so much better than theirs. As I reflected on how good God had been to me, it came home to me how many other youths were in the same predicament as those two troubled teenagers. (And still are.) I wanted to give them something that would lift them up and give them hope for the future. And the best thing I could possibly do for them, I knew, was introduce them to the love and power of Jesus Christ.

If I had to pinpoint a time in my life when the conviction was born that God wanted me to return to Mississippi, I would point to that morning. But in the days and weeks that followed, the urgency grew within me. It captured my thoughts during the day. It kept me awake at night. God was not asking me; He was *commanding* me to go home and share the Gospel with my people.

I was drawn to the words of the apostle Paul: "Brethren, my heart's desire and prayer to God for Israel is that they may be saved. For I bear them witness that they have a zeal for God, but not according to knowledge" (Romans 10:1–2). As surely as the great apostle grieved for the lost souls of his native Israel, I grieved for the lost and hopeless souls of my native Mississippi.

I knew from personal experience that many of the black churches of Mississippi (and throughout the South) had a zeal for God, but with little knowledge. For far too many Southern blacks, Christianity was a Sunday morning thing—a few hours of emotion and feeling good—that had little to do with life the rest of the week. They knew little or nothing in the way of discipleship, nor did they understand many of the Gospel's implications regarding the equality of all people.

I will take that a step further.

In the black South of that day, the preacher was a powerful figure—perhaps the most powerful man in the entire community. Much of the time he was able to hold that important position only because he had the backing of the white community. Most of these men pastored three, four, even five churches, visiting each only once per month. This system worked well for them. Many drove big, fancy cars and lived far away. Whatever the preacher said, that was the way it was. These men had little interest in changing the status quo, and it was easy to see why. They were treated with respect and even awe by church members and community residents.

This is what Vera Mae and I faced in 1960 when I felt God calling me (and that meant us) to return to Mississippi.

Now, Vera Mae and I had four children by this time, with a fifth one soon on the way, so I am sure you can understand when I tell you that Vera Mae was not the least bit enthusiastic about my revelation.

I am sure she hoped it was just a passing fancy that would soon be forgotten. Much to my surprise, most of my newfound Christian friends reacted the same way. They knew I had a passion for reaching the lost but saw no reason why I could not fulfill that passion right there in southern California. They did not want me to do anything rash.

Only a few friends agreed with me that going back to the South was a good thing to do. I felt somewhat isolated and lonely. And then, to top it all off, I got sick. Deathly sick.

Doctors could not figure out what was wrong with me, but I was wasting away. It seemed like every time I stepped on the scale, a few more pounds had come off. But whenever the doctors thought they had figured out what was wrong with me, it turned out they were running down another dead-end street. In a few months I lost more than forty pounds, I was feeling terribly weak and run down, as if I had one foot in the grave—and none of the doctors could figure out why.

What I did not know was that all that time God had been speaking to Vera Mae—very pregnant, as I said, with our fifth child—about His desire for me to take the Gospel back to Mississippi. The more I had talked about it, the more she had dug in her heels to prevent it. But God had been telling her that if she did not let me go, she might lose me altogether, and she did not want that to happen.

Finally one day in November I was too weak to get out of bed. When I tried, I found I could not even stand up. It was looking like the beginning of the end. I just lay there staring at the ceiling and wondering what was going to happen to me. Then I saw Vera Mae tiptoe into the room.

When she saw that I was awake, she announced, "Toop, I'm going to pray for you." (I should tell you that when I was a boy, my nickname was Tupy, and Vera Mae has always called me Toop.) Then she knelt down by the side of the bed.

"Lord," she began, "it's a hard struggle for me to say yes, but I'm going to say yes. I'm willing to go to Mississippi. I don't want to go, but I'm willing. Lord, I'm saying yes to You."

That was not the entire prayer. There was a lot more, asking God to raise me up and make me strong so that I could be the husband and father I had always been. But I am afraid my attention did not get very far past the part where she finally gave up and said she was willing to go back home to Mississippi.

By the time Vera Mae had finished praying, she told me later, she felt much better. In fact, the moment she told God she was willing to do whatever He asked, she felt the burden lift from her shoulders.

I felt better, too. I was still too weak to stand up, but I was at peace. I knew I was going to be all right. I also knew we were going to Mississippi.

The next day, incredibly, I felt strong enough to get out of bed. Immediately I began making plans for a trip down South, just to check it out. It was not the best time to be away from home, I knew, since it was only a few days before Thanksgiving. Besides, the doctors still did not know what was wrong with me, and advised me to take it easy. But I was determined to go now, and that's what I did.

A very pregnant Vera Mae and the children took me down to the station, said good-bye and put me on the bus for Mississippi. I did not even know what I was going to do when I got there.

Well, I spent the next six weeks checking things out—preaching in different churches around New Hebron, sharing with the people what I felt God calling me to do, looking for the right location to begin my ministry. Slowly but steadily I began to regain all the weight I had lost. My strength returned. I felt energetic, enthusiastic and excited.

To this day, I still do not know what had been wrong with me. But whatever it was, God healed me completely. Furthermore, what I saw during those six weeks in Mississippi made me more certain than ever that this was where God was calling me to be.

At the same time, I was convinced that the task that lay before me was not going to be easy. I was not the least bit frightened about things—but I did have my eyes wide open.

I took a long, cold bus ride back to California in December, getting home on Christmas Eve.

I am sure that deep down inside, Vera Mae was still hoping I would tell her I had changed my mind—that God wanted us to stay in California after all. But she was willing and ready to do what God wanted, and she was also willing for God to reveal His will to and through me.

She did not show the least bit of disappointment or reluctance when I reaffirmed to her my commitment to relocate to Mississippi. So we both went about the details of getting ready to make the move. We prepared to quit our jobs. We put our house up for rent. Our Christian friends rallied around us with prayer and financial support.

By June 6, 1960, all the loose ends had been tied up. We packed our children in the car—including little Deborah, who had been born in January—and headed east on Route 66.

It was strange and kind of disheartening to find out how little attitudes in Mississippi had changed in the thirteen-plus years we had been away. Any changes that had come had been forced by the federal government and not been accepted enthusiastically by the people—or, I should say, the white people. The hearts of the vast majority of Mississippi's white residents had not changed. They were pro-segregation, pro-white superiority and anti-black. Yes, there were exceptions, but it was immediately clear to me that racism was alive and healthy in Dixie.

It was also clear that conditions in the black community had not changed much either. Sometimes I had the distinct impression, looking around me, that I had been transported to a third-world country. I saw rampant unemployment, crushing poverty, illiteracy, crime and hopelessness. People were living in houses without running water or electricity, without glass in the windows, with hole-filled roofs and walls that could not begin to keep out the wind or rain. I saw people who had no way to heat their houses during the coldest winter days (and it *does* get cold in Mississippi, even if it is 'way down South). I saw people who did not have enough food to eat and who never went to a doctor themselves or took their children to a doctor, no matter how sick they were. They just could not afford it.

There was one new element, however, in many of the communities: the school.

You see, Mississippi was still trying to prove to the rest of the world that it was possible to have "separate but equal" facilities, including schools, for blacks and whites. So over the years prior to 1960, the state had poured quite a bit of money into building new schools in many black areas. It was really a public relations campaign to make segregation look better, of course, but at least the black community benefited from it.

I decided that the school-building boom gave me a good place to begin my ministry in the state. So that fall, when Vera Mae and I registered our children in school, I asked the principal about the possibility of conducting some regular Bible classes. He thought that was a fine idea, so I began teaching Bible classes in the school at New Hymn, near Pinola. Things went so well there that I was soon teaching classes in six adjacent counties. I also became the regular chaplain at Prentiss Institute, a black junior college. My talk there during spiritual emphasis week resulted in about forty students accepting Christ.

The next few years were times of readjustment and trial for our family—but we were happy because we knew we were doing what God wanted us to do. Even the youngest of our children seemed to feel that way, and there was almost no whining or complaining, even though life was different for us now. We were missionaries, after all, and wanted to live alongside the people we were serving—experience the same conditions they lived in, share their sorrows and discomforts, share their hopes and dreams.

As the various Bible classes continued, we bought a huge tent that we took from town to town locally, spending at least two weeks in each place. We were not like some tent-toting evangelists touring the South in those days in that we were not interested in putting on a glitzy show. We were interested only in preaching and teaching the Word of God, giving a biblical foundation to people who had lived for years on little more than emotion.

Response was even better than we hoped for. Everywhere we went, good crowds came to hear the Gospel—as many as 150 every night, and sometimes more than that. Folks who were "hungering and thirsting" for God and His righteousness found their way into our tent.

We were thrilled with the response, but it quickly became apparent that we needed a permanent central location. And so, with $900 from my savings account, I bought five small lots in the black section of the town of Mendenhall, on which we built a house. Several young men who attended our Bible classes helped us finish the house, which would serve as the center of our outreach to the community, and as the Perkins family's living quarters.

It was pretty to look at. But no paved street into the area. No hookups to sewers or other utilities. One thing I had discovered, though, was that we needed a visible presence in the community. This building was a sign to the people that we planned to be here permanently, and that anyone who needed us would know where to find us. It was important that they consider us their friends and partners.

Because of the deplorable conditions in which many of them lived, we knew right away that it was not enough just to preach to them. They did need to know, of course, that Jesus loved them. But they needed to see His love manifested in someone willing to work alongside them to help them change things for themselves and their children.

They needed to know that Jesus loved them so much that He wanted them to have a sense of personal dignity and self-respect; that He wanted them to be treated the same as *any* self-respecting person would expect to be treated.

They needed to know that Jesus loved them so much that He wanted them to have decent housing to live in; that He wanted them to have jobs so they could provide for their families; that He wanted them and their children to be well-fed and healthy; that He did not want them to have to huddle together in their houses in order to live through the winter.

That was our plan from the start—not only to tell them about the love of God, but to show them God's love by helping them change their lives for the better. It is important to add that we were not planning on doing things for these people. We wanted to work with them so they could help themselves. And who could have a problem with that?

As it turned out, lots of people.

And not only in Mississippi.

My efforts to change things in our community earned me a reputation as a troublemaker in the eyes of some Mississippi whites. I expected that. But I did not expect to be questioned by some of my white friends and supporters in California, who wondered out loud if I was getting away from the preaching of the Gospel and into politics. I tried to show them from the Scriptures that God's love encompasses every facet of a person's being—physical, emotional and spiritual—but they had a difficult time understanding that. I had to conclude that they just did not understand what life was like for our people in Mississippi.

Suppose you were a black man living in a town like Mendenhall and you got so sick you decided you had to go to the clinic, even though you might be hard-pressed to pay for the doctor's services. When you get to the clinic, you find two waiting rooms—one for whites and one for blacks. You can be sure that every person in that white waiting room is going to see the doctor before you have a chance of being seen. It might be hours before you get in to see the doctor, and you might even die in the meantime.

That is typical of the kind of treatment we faced in many different areas of our lives. I felt that Christian love would compel a person to speak out against that kind of injustice, no matter what the color of his skin. But too many white Christians seemed to shrug their shoulders and say, "That's just the way it is." Surely, I thought, if they had been in my place, they would have done what I was doing.

Would they not?

It made me sad that people who were so generous when it came to providing money for Bibles and teaching materials were reluctant to give money to help feed a poor child or help fix a hole in the roof so a family could stay dry and warm. Clearly people did not understand the fullness of the Gospel.

I did not understand then—and I do not understand now—how people can claim to be concerned about someone's eternal state but not be the least bit interested in the hardships he or she is suffering in this life. It just does not make sense. Throughout the years there has been a lot of talk about "the social gospel" as opposed to the "real" Gospel, and that is a tragedy, because when we touch a man with the Gospel, we will touch every area of his being. A poor person will be lifted up and shown that he is a creature of dignity and worth, someone created in the image of God, someone for whom Christ died. A rich man will be compelled by the love of Christ to use his money to lift up the less fortunate and touch them with God's love.

One of the ways we were prevented from improving our lives in the South in the 1960s was being kept out of the political process. Even though we supposedly had the right to vote, a number of state laws conspired to stop us.

There was the poll tax of two dollars. That does not sound like much money, especially today, but two dollars back then was equal to fifteen or twenty dollars today, and it was not easy for most blacks to come up with an extra couple of dollars. Then, too, if the would-be voter did come up with the money, the sheriff, who often doubled as the poll-tax collector, could simply come up with some reason to refuse the money.

Then there was the literacy test. The prospective voter would be asked to fill out a questionnaire asking for extensive personal information, including his family history. Then he or she would be asked to read a section of the state constitution and write a thorough explanation of what had been read. He or she might be asked, for instance, to read and interpret this passage from Section 182 of the Mississippi constitution:

> The power to tax corporations and their property shall never be surrendered or abridged by any contract or grant to which the state or any political subdivision thereof may be a party, except that the legislature may grant exemption from taxation in the encouragement of manufacturers and other new enterprises of public utility extending for a period of not exceeding five years, the time of such exemptions to commence from date of charter, if to a corporation; and if to an individual enterprise, then from the commencement of work; but when the legislature grants such exemptions for a period of five years or less, it shall be done by general laws, which shall distinctly enumerate the classes of manufacturers and other new enterprises of public utility entitled to such exemptions, and shall prescribe the mode and manner in which the right to such exemptions shall be determined.

Even if the prospective voter could understand and interpret such sections correctly, it was still up to a white registrar to decide whether the answer was good enough to earn a voter registration card—and there was simply no pleasing some white registrars.

No wonder so few blacks were able to vote!

But without the vote, we had no chance of removing from office white sheriffs and other officials who were openly antagonistic toward us.

And without the vote, there was no way for us to challenge the political power structure. We could not vote into office men and women who would be more concerned about issues that affected our community. Why should the white politician care if the black community's streets were run-down, if the schools were poorly maintained, if we had problems with crime or if city services were sorely lacking? If we did not even vote, why should he answer to us?

It was for all these reasons that I became deeply involved in voter registration drives throughout Mississippi. Several of our community leaders got together and chose representatives to head up voter registration drives in various parts of the state. I was selected to be the representative for Simpson, Lawrence and parts of Rankin and Smith Counties.

Because the federal government was heavily involved in trying to open up the political process in Mississippi, the Justice Department assigned some people to work with us. We visited the polling places to make sure they were equally accessible to whites and blacks, we accompanied blacks when they went to register to vote and so on.

I remember clearly how fearful some of the Justice Department people seemed to be. And with good reason. They were putting their lives on the line. So was I, even though I did not think about it much at the time. But the men from the Justice Department were putting themselves in greater danger, because if there was anyone Mississippi whites hated, it was "outside agitators." A white man trying to help blacks gain political equality was often seen as a traitor. A traitor was not fit to live.

And folks in Mississippi had ways of spotting traitors.

If a white man was driving a nice car, for instance, and he had a black man as a passenger, that *might* be O.K. After all, that was the way it was supposed to be, with the white man "in charge." But if a black man was driving a nice car and the white man was a passenger, both of them were suspect. It was figured that more than likely they were civil rights workers, and civil rights workers were fair game.

I saw some white civil rights workers spat on, slapped, kicked, shoved and called names that I would not possibly repeat. I saw them treated with a violent contempt that I had never seen directed at a black person. In fact, I was amazed when I saw how some of them put up with the abuse and kept trying to do their jobs.

Right from the beginning in Mississippi, I took the attitude of treating people with respect, and I expected to be treated the same way. Respect, as far as I was concerned, meant meeting people on an equal footing. It did not mean shuffling around and mumbling "yassah" and "no'm" and keeping a plastic smile spread across my face. I was not belligerent and did not go around with a chip on my shoulder, but I looked people in the eye when I spoke to them and held myself erect, since I was not ashamed of who I was.

There were white people who did not like that very much. What I saw as simple self-respect, they saw as arrogance and considered me to be "uppity."

I remember one occasion, for example, when I drove into a service station and got ready to begin pumping gas into my car. I do not know what it was about my manner that irritated the attendant so much, but he came over and began cursing and calling me a nigger. Perhaps he was angry because I was going about the business of pumping my own gas the way any self-respecting white person would have done.

But whatever his problem was, I was not going to stand there and take that abuse. I just hung the hose back on the pump and drove off, watching the man in the rear-view mirror as he continued with his temper tantrum.

Well, if my attitude alone was not enough to convince the white bigots in my community that I was a troublemaker, my work in behalf of voter registration certainly did the trick.

When we began our voter registration efforts in Simpson County, there were only fifty black voters in the whole county. In one summer we managed to register a thousand more, then continued the effort until we had more than 2,300 blacks on the voter rolls.

That may have been cause for rejoicing in the black community, but it was a threat to the white power structure. Just how much of a threat was seen in a 1968 election, when a former schoolteacher named William "Shag" Pyron was elected as Southern District Commissioner of the Mississippi Highway Commission, upsetting an incumbent who had held the post for twenty years. What made Pyron's election upsetting to the white establishment was that he had promised to open up highway department jobs to blacks, whereas his opponent, John Smith, was an open racist. It was obvious to everyone that Pyron's election came about only because of black support.

So it was that we began to receive increasingly violent pamphlets and other racist materials in the mail, and threats over the telephone.

"Perkins is a troublemaker," one voice said. "He could get himself killed."

Another voice warned Vera Mae, "Mrs. Perkins, you don't want to be a widow, do you?"

And another: "Reverend Perkins is as good as dead right now. You better get out of town fast!"

We took the threats seriously but were determined not to let them stop us from doing what we knew God wanted us to do. We were determined to continue, despite increasing Klan activity throughout Mississippi, including bombings of black churches, murders of some black activists and suspicious cars driving slowly past our house in the middle of the night.

My greatest fear was not for myself but for Vera Mae and the children. My ministry often took me out of town, sometimes for days at a time, and I always worried about leaving my family at home alone. I did not know what the Ku Klux Klan might do, but I would not have been surprised by anything.

Early one morning when I was away, Vera Mae thought she heard something in front of the house, so she got out of bed and turned on the light. Immediately she heard the squealing of tires and the sound of gravel being sprayed down the street in front of the house. She got to the window in time to see an old pickup speeding around the corner. From the sound when the truck first took off, Vera Mae was certain that the truck had been parked right beside our car. She felt sure that whoever was in it had been trying to plant a bomb in our car.

She called the local police, who said someone would be right out to investigate. It would have taken no more than five minutes for a patrol car to get to our house, but none ever came. She waited a half hour, then an hour, and finally decided that if she wanted help, she would have to get the federal authorities. So she called the FBI office in Jackson. They said they would send someone out right away, and told her not to touch the car until he got there.

Not one to let even a bomb threat disturb her usual routine, Vera Mae borrowed a neighbor's car to take the children to school, then came home and waited for the agent.

He got there about nine o'clock. Vera Mae watched from the house as he crawled underneath the car. Apparently finding nothing there, he opened the door gently, got inside and crawled under the dash. Finally he popped open the hood.

Nothing. The agent was visibly relieved, and so was Vera Mae. Apparently she had surprised the men in the truck before they had been able to finish whatever it was they were planning to do.

Maybe they had a bomb. Or maybe they just wanted us think they had a bomb. Whichever it was, the FBI agent told Vera Mae to let him know if she noticed anything else suspicious, and that if she called, he would be at our place just as fast as he could get there.

In the days and weeks that followed, there was plenty of suspicious activity, including strange pickup trucks with gun racks driving slowly past our house at all hours of the night. I finally decided that I had to do something, so I called a Sunday night meeting at our church to discuss the situation.

The building was packed with friends who wanted to help defend us against Klan terror. I was almost overcome as I looked out over the sea of determined faces and thought how far some of these people had come. There was a dignity and unity here, and I loved them with my whole heart.

For the next several nights, our house was guarded by groups of black men. They watched and waited and listened. We prayed that there would be no confrontation, because we did not want violence . . . but we were prepared for it if it came.

For a while the entire community seemed perched on the edge of a race war.

But an open confrontation was not at all what the Klan was looking for. They preferred isolated acts of terror to open confrontation. They were anxious to fight only when they clearly outnumbered their opponents. A fair fight was against everything they stood for.

So after a while the Klansmen and their supporters slunk back into the darkness and we were left alone.

It was quiet—but a storm was coming.

War!

Tom Tarrants

I was still a young man, barely out of my teens, when I met Sam Bowers, imperial wizard of the White Knights.

I was a thoroughly indoctrinated, well-trained fanatic, willing to put my life on the line in defense of "the cause." I was even willing to take actions that might injure others. This was war, and war meant casualties.

Bowers was an intelligent, thoughtful man who fancied himself an intellectual.

As I look back on it now, it is hard to square Bowers' intelligence with his absolute belief in an international Jewish conspiracy, or with his antagonism toward those whose only "crime" was that their skin was a different color than his. But that is the way Sam Bowers saw the world.

Bowers actually looked down on the "redneck" Southerners who made up the vast majority of his White Knights of the Ku Klux Klan. They did not know a thing about political theory. Most of them did not even know there was a worldwide conspiracy; all they knew was, they hated Jews and blacks. Bowers was more than happy to use their unreasoning hatred to further his own agenda.

It was about a three-hour drive from my home in Mobile to Bowers' Sambo Amusement Company in Laurel, Mississippi. I made the drive one day, knocked on Bowers' door and introduced myself. I told him I was going to apply for a job at the Masonite Corporation there in Laurel, had heard of him and was very impressed by the White Knights' effectiveness. I told him something of my views and we parted.

I liked the White Knights' style and I liked Bowers' style.

The White Knights, for example, had once planted a bomb on Bowers' orders in the offices of Laurel's daily newspaper, *The Leader-Call*, even though the paper had not said one harsh word about the Klan. After the bombing, Bowers sent word to the newspaper's editor that the blast was "not for anything you did to us, but because you did not do anything for us."

At first Bowers was suspicious of me. And not without reason. Bowers could not be certain whether he was talking to a true patriot or an FBI informant. It was difficult for anyone in the Klan to trust anyone else in the Klan. For one thing, an organization built around mistrust and hatred of those outside its membership is not likely to be peaceful and harmonious on the inside, either. For another thing, FBI informants were everywhere. Besides, Bowers' personality entered into it. He did not let many people get close to him. But I contacted him again for further talks. I think he began to see that I had a "correct understanding" of what was going on in the world, and that I was sold out to the cause.

True, I had not graduated with my high school class, but that was not because I had had any academic trouble in school. Rather, I did not intend to waste my time sitting in a classroom learning things like geometry and ancient history while our society was being destroyed from within. I had more important things to learn, and over the past few years had been learning it, submerging myself in political theory, revolutionary tactics and guerrilla warfare. I drew my passion and strength from the writings of those who had given themselves entirely to the cause. Adolf Hitler was one of my heroes, as was Robert E. Lee. Though indescribably different from one another, these were men truly committed to their cause.

Ironically, the way I felt about the cause of the radical right was eloquently expressed in a letter an American Communist wrote to his fiancée years ago. Although I hated Communists, I had the same devotion to my cause.

> We Communists suffer many casualties. We are those whom they shoot, hang, lynch, tar and feather, imprison, slander, fire from our jobs and whose lives people make miserable in every way possible. Some of us are killed and imprisoned. We live in poverty. From what we earn we turn over to the Party every cent which we do not absolutely need to live.
>
> We Communists have neither time nor money to go to movies very often, nor for concerts, nor for beautiful homes and new cars. They call us fanatics. We are fanatics. Our lives are dominated by one supreme factor—the struggle for world Communism. We Communists have a philosophy of life that money could not buy. We have a cause to fight for, a specific goal in life. We lose our insignificant identities in the great river of humanity; and if our personal lives seem hard, or if our egos seem bruised through subordination to the Party, we are amply rewarded—in the thought that all of us, even though it be in a very small way, are contributing something new and better for humanity.
>
> There is one thing about which I am completely in earnest—the Communist cause. It is my life, my business, my religion, my hobby, my sweetheart, my wife, my mistress, my meat and drink. I work at it by day and dream of it by night. Its control over me grows greater with the passage of time. Therefore I cannot have a friend, a lover or even a conversation without relating them to this power that animates and controls my life. I measure people, books, ideas and deeds according to the way they affect the Communist cause and by their attitude to it. I have already been in jail for my ideas, and if need be, I am ready to face death.

That is exactly how I felt about what I was doing. I also agreed with Robert Shelton, imperial wizard of the United Klans of America, who wrote in *The Fiery Cross:*

> We have given the Negroes an education, and what outcome have we reaped? Thousands and hundreds of thousands of Negro MORONS, THICK LIPPED, BULGY EYED, WINED UP, DOPED UP MORONS . . . laboring under the delusion that they have an education which makes them the equal of our white race. . . .

Yes, the Negro may wear a Palm Beach suit instead of the beads he stole from a neighboring village, he may carry a gold headed cane instead of a shrunken head, and he may use the telephone instead of his ancient drum, but is his MIND any less than that of a savage? And my friends, MIND is the man, for as a man thinketh, so he is, contrary to Karl Marx's theory that "a man is what he eats." The Negroes have been eating humans for years . . . but they are still animals!

I have no race prejudices, my friends . . . for what the fools call race prejudice is the God implanted instinct of self preservation, the first law of nature.

There is not a hope, in faith or in reason, for the Negro outside of complete and total separation. . . .

On our side are the forces of freedom, liberty, racial integrity and white supremacy, led by the United Klans of America. On the other side are the forces of communism, Black Nationalism, Socialism, which all come under the index of WORLD ZIONISM, the force that is using all these by-products to accomplish their objective.

Combine the dedication of the Communist with the hatred expressed by Robert Shelton and you have a dangerous combination. That is exactly what I had—and that is why Sam Bowers and I got along so well.

Another thing that brought Bowers and me together was the fact that we were both religious.

I had made a profession of faith and been baptized when I was thirteen—mainly because I was afraid of going to hell when I died. Other than relieving my fear, the experience had not changed my life at all. I believed in teachings about Christ but knew nothing of repentance and the new birth. But I never doubted my "salvation." Like many then and now, I claimed to be a Christian while my actions disproved it.

Bowers was also religious. He knew the Scriptures and sprinkled his conversation with quotes from the Bible. He prayed. He looked forward to the Second Coming of Christ.

And he saw no inconsistency between his personal faith and his involvement in the murders of innocent people. He put it this way:

"As Christians we are disposed to kindness, generosity, affection and humility in our dealings with others. As militants we are disposed to use physical force against our enemies. How can we reconcile these two apparently contradictory philosophies? The answer, of course, is to purge malice, bitterness and vengeance from our hearts."

He also said, "If it is necessary to eliminate someone, it should be done with no malice, in complete silence and in the manner of a Christian act."

Bowers thought, in other words, that it was perfectly acceptable to lynch a man or blow up his house with him in it as long as you did it with the right motives and in the right way.

Bowers was also careful to cover his tracks, and was wary of being seen with anyone who might be under suspicion by the FBI. He was always afraid that the FBI might be listening to our conversations via some bug they had hidden in his office, telephone or car. So we met in a variety of strange places to plan our activities and conducted phone conversations that would have been unintelligible to anyone who did not know the code we used.

Usually we met in a wooded area outside of Laurel. We drove in separate cars, then got out and walked deep into the woods, as far away from prying eyes and ears as possible.

On one occasion, late one night, we were brave enough to meet in Bowers' office. We did not talk at all but carried on our conversation in writing, handing a notebook back and forth. Even that was not enough protection for Bowers. When we were done "talking," he burned the pages with our notes on them, ground up the ashes and we flushed them down the toilet. Even after all that, I am not sure he felt completely safe.

This kind of fear and paranoia over FBI penetration and surveillance was a major hindrance to our activities. Had it been otherwise, I have no doubt but that there would have been much more Klan violence in the late 1960s. As it was, there was plenty.

In September 1967 the Klan launched a full-scale terrorist attack against Jews, blacks and white civil rights workers. The target was anyone who disagreed with us—or at least anyone who disagreed with us openly.

The first attack came on September 18 when an explosive device was detonated at Temple Beth Israel in Jackson. The blast, which according to news accounts rattled windows in homes up to a quarter of a mile from the synagogue, blew out the front double doors of the building, buckled walls and shattered windows.

The White Knights of the Ku Klux Klan—Sam Bowers and me included—were delighted. The only negative aspect of the bombing, as far as we could see, was that no Jews were killed or injured. Still, we knew that a powerful message had been sent to every Jew in Mississippi.

The Klan's next attack was aimed at the black community. The specific target: Tougaloo College, a black institution just outside of Jackson. Tougaloo students were active in the civil rights movement throughout the South—active, among other things, in the protests led by the Rev. John Perkins—and we considered the college to be an important part of the Jewish-Communist struggle in Mississippi. And so, early in the morning on October 6, an explosive device did substantial damage to the home of Dr. William T. Bush, the dean of the college.

Other bombings followed in quick succession.

Having bombed a Jewish synagogue and the on-campus house of a black college dean, the White Knights needed to send a message to whites sympathetic to the civil rights movement. The target was Robert Kochtitzky, a Jackson resident who had spoken out on behalf of civil rights for blacks and who had been openly and harshly critical of the Klan following the bombing of Temple Beth Israel.

The Kochtitzky bombing narrowly missed injuring or killing his wife and infant son, who were sleeping in the house at the time. Nevertheless, the bombing did not achieve its desired effect. Kochtitzky did not stop supporting the civil rights movement, nor did he stop criticizing the Klan.

In fact, some of the area's white preachers, most of whom had remained silent in the face of the Klan's increasing violence, now spoke out against the Klan and Klan violence. They had been sitting on the fence, so to speak, but the latest bombing had pushed them into action. They felt they could no longer be passive spectators. They had to get involved.

From the perspective of the White Knights, that was not so bad. We were surprised and disgusted, of course, that anyone claiming to preach the Gospel could actively support those attempting to overthrow our God-fearing country. At the same time, we had a clearer idea now of who our enemies were, and figured that if they thought we were being too violent now, they had not seen anything yet.

The next target was the home of a black minister, the Rev. Allan Johnson, who lived in the community of Laurel, Mississippi, was a former assistant state director of the National Association for the Advancement of Colored People and was also widely known throughout the state for his involvement with the Southern Christian Leadership Conference.

On November 21, just after eleven at night, a bomb exploded at the home of Rabbi Perry Nussbaum of Temple Beth Israel. This was yet another message to the Jewish community that the Klan had declared war on them and their race-mixing schemes.

Nothing further happened until just before Christmas. Then, on a cold and rainy day, Sam Bowers and I decided to take a twenty-minute drive from Laurel to the Mississippi town of Collins to pay a visit to a black man who had recently been arrested and charged with shooting at a policeman.

We had a loaded submachine gun and planned to use it. But we got lost and pulled into the parking lot of a closed service station to see if we could get our bearings. Almost immediately a police car pulled in behind us. The officer got out, came up to the driver's side of the car and asked to see my driver's license. He wanted to know who we were and what we were doing in Collins. He was suspicious because my car had Alabama tags and, more than that, it was unusual for two white men to be cruising through the "black part of town." I do not remember exactly what we told him, but our answers were not good enough and he decided to take us in for questioning.

While we were in jail, a search of my car turned up the loaded submachine gun, which had been concealed under a sweater on the front seat. Furthermore, a check of the serial number of my car revealed that it had been stolen several months earlier.

Because Bowers was widely known as the leader of the White Knights, and because he was already under indictment for murder, it seemed certain that we would be locked up for a while. Nevertheless, we were released on bond the following day, with a trial date set for early spring.

I enrolled in classes in a local Baptist college back home in Mobile, hoping that a better image would help me beat the charges. (Earlier I had completed the requirements for a high school equivalency certificate.) But as the trial date drew closer, I became more and more convinced that there was no way I could be found innocent. I was clearly guilty and certain I would be sent to jail, probably for a long time. I also knew I would be no good to the cause sitting behind bars.

I decided to go underground, and set out for California.

In California I spent a week with Wesley Swift, whose teaching had influenced me over the previous two years and whom I held in high regard. I learned from him and his aide, Dennis Mowrer, who was the West Coast coordinator of the Minutemen, another right-wing paramilitary organization. While there I also met Richard Butler, a Swift follower, now head of the Aryan Nation movement. I took advantage of every moment with Swift and Mowrer, picking their brains with regard to strategy and ideology. Afterward I decided to spend a few days with a favorite uncle who lived in San Diego.

That visit was strange, to say the least. I had absolutely nothing in common with my uncle or his family, and I wondered what had happened to them. They seemed interested in silly things like the weather, the state of the economy and the non-news that filled the pages of the morning newspaper. They did not have a clue as to what was *really* happening in the world. Didn't they know there was a war going on, that that war was the only thing worth thinking or talking about?

The truth was, I was so changed, so consumed by "the cause," that I no longer had anything in common with people I had once loved dearly. I had nothing in common with anyone who did not share my obsession.

After a few days in San Diego, I decided it was time to go home to Mobile and take my chances at being caught.

I should have known it was too late to go home. FBI agents were staked out in front of my house, waiting to arrest me on sight. I saw them sitting in their car as soon as I turned onto my street. Maybe if I just kept going as nonchalantly as possible, I thought, they would not recognize me.

It didn't work. The federal agents spotted me almost as quickly as I had spotted them. What saved me was that their car was facing the opposite direction from mine and their engine was not running. I stomped my accelerator to the floor and sped off down the street. Looking into my rear-view mirror, I saw them trying to turn their car around.

A quick right turn onto this street . . . a left turn onto that one . . . a few more turns . . . and I had left them far behind.

I felt a strong sense of exhilaration—not because I had lost them, but because I now knew there was no turning back. The battle lines had been drawn more clearly than ever.

I made plans to travel to North Carolina, where I would stay with a family that had ties to Wesley Swift and other extreme right-wing organizations. The house was located in the mountains near the small town of Franklin, where there was plenty of room for target practice.

It was at this time that I wrote the following "memo," which I carried with me everywhere I went:

Gentlemen:
Please be advised that as of March 23, 1968, I, Thomas Albert Tarrants, III, was forced to go underground or be arrested and imprisoned on framed Federal charges of violation of National Firearms Act and other misc. charges. My decision to make this announcement was in part influenced by a similar announcement by that great patriot Robert DePugh of the Minutemen. In that my situation is very similar to his, I have decided to make public this announcement.

I will further state that I have always believed in military action against the common enemy. I have committed myself totally to defeating the Communist Jew conspiracy which threatens our country—any means necessary shall be used. On March 23, 1968, I was forced to go underground or face framed federal charges of possession of a submachine gun in Collins, Mississippi, on 21 December 1967.

Please be advised that since March 28, 1968, I, Thomas A. Tarrants, have been underground and operating guerrilla warfare.

From my base in North Carolina, I made several trips back to Mississippi to meet with Klan leaders. By this time there were hundreds of FBI agents in Mississippi, but the Klan terror continued unabated. In the community of Meridian alone, there were eleven terrorist attacks between January and May, including the burning of eight black churches and a powerful blast that caused several thousands dollars' worth of damage to a Jewish synagogue.

In June 1968 I came back from North Carolina to finalize the plans for a very important mission: the bombing of Meyer Davidson's house.

My days as a "soldier" were about to end.

Into the Maelstrom

John Perkins

White people unite.
Defeat Jew/Communist race mixers.

That friendly sign stood alongside Highway 49, welcoming visitors to the town of Mendenhall.

I had driven past it so many times it usually did not make me wince. But today it hurt. It hurt because it was just a few days before Christmas, a time of peace and brotherhood, and the sign—which I had come to take almost for granted—seemed jarringly out of context. (Especially when the thought hit me that the sign was undoubtedly erected by a God-fearing individual who thought of himself as a good Christian.)

The sign also hurt because it was directed at good young men like the one who sat beside me in the driver's seat of the Volkswagen beetle, Doug Huemmer.

Doug was a college-age kid from California who had come to Mendenhall to help in the work of Voice of Calvary Ministries (the outgrowth of a church we had started). He was one of a number of young white volunteers who had come to help us with the task of improving our community. And when I say task, I mean task. Doug had worked extremely hard. He was a good guy, and I really appreciated him.

Not too many of the white folks in Mendenhall shared my opinion. They did not like Doug because they saw him as one of those

84

"Jew/Communist race mixers." They did not like me either, of course. Most of the white folks in town treated us as if we were criminals.

What had we done that was so terrible?

We had started Bible classes in a number of schools throughout the state of Mississippi.

We had started pre-school programs to give disadvantaged youngsters a chance to succeed in school.

We had started co-op programs that repaired dilapidated housing on the poor side of town and provided poor farmers with the ability to increase their crops and become self-sufficient.

We had helped thousands of American citizens register to vote so they could be more involved in the democratic process.

That does not sound like a list of crimes that would attract the attention of the FBI, but it was enough if you lived in the American South and you were black, or if the people you were helping were black.

Doug and I were on our way to a small grocery store so he could buy a bottle of country cane syrup, which he planned to give to his parents for Christmas. He was going home for the holidays—flying out of Jackson that night, as a matter of fact—and wanted to give his parents something that was "pure South."

It was nearly dark by the time we got to the little store, and there was a bit of a ruckus going on inside. A young black man, Garland Wilks, was involved in a heated discussion with the white clerk. It quickly became apparent that Garland was angry because he could not get the clerk to accept his check for the few items he was buying. It was also apparent that Garland had been drinking. He was not drunk, but I knew very well that the local police did not need much of an excuse to brutalize a "drunk nigger." This little ruckus, unless somebody did something, could become a major disaster.

"Garland," I said, "how about letting us give you a ride home?"

He was not sure, but I persisted. "Come on, you don't need all this stuff. Let's go."

To my surprise, the young man was willing to let go of the fight. Doug and I guided him outside, helped him into the back seat of the car and headed off in the direction of his house. We were both feeling relieved that we had been able to avert a major problem.

We did not know that the storekeeper had already called the police. He was angry and wanted Garland arrested.

Doug looked in his rearview mirror. "Uh-oh."

I turned around. A police car was right behind us.

I was nervous. Then I thought, *Maybe he's not really after us. After all, he hasn't turned his lights on.*

It was as if the policeman had read my thoughts. Those flashing lights came on almost immediately.

Doug pulled quickly to the side of the road, and he and I jumped out of the car to ask what was wrong.

Both policemen got out of their car, too. They were not happy. "You just shut up!" one of them yelled at Doug. "Stand aside!"

The other policeman stuck his head inside the door of the VW.

"You come out of there, Garland," he demanded. "You're under arrest."

"Under arrest?" I asked. "For what?"

"For public drunkenness and disturbing the peace."

"But he's in the car with us. He's not disturbing the peace."

"You just shut up!" the cop shot back.

It was not my intention to make the policemen mad. That would not be good for Garland or for Doug and me. But Garland had not meant any harm, and I was afraid of what might happen to him if he was taken into custody. Lately I had been hearing a lot of stories about police brutality against blacks. Although I did not believe everything I heard, I had seen enough on my own to know there was at least some truth behind the stories. I knew for a fact that there had been a number of arrests on trumped-up charges (disturbing the peace was a favorite) and that some blacks had been beaten while in police custody. I also knew that most local police and sheriff's departments in Mississippi were full of Klansmen and Klan sympathizers who liked nothing better than an excuse to bust open a black man's head.

But there was nothing further we could do to protect Garland, so he meekly obeyed the policeman's command to "come out of there," and he was put into the back seat of the patrol car.

Doug and I went on to Voice of Calvary, where a group of our high school and college-age students was rehearsing a Christmas pageant. Things were already in an uproar there over another arrest that had occurred earlier that day. It seemed a young man named Roy Berry had been arrested and beaten, reportedly because he was suspected of making harassing phone calls to a white woman, asking her for a date.

"They beat him real bad, Reverend Perkins," one of the young women sobbed. "They told him they ought to kill him. And now they're gonna beat up Garland, too."

I knew she was probably right. But what could we do about it? If I went down to the police station, they would probably arrest and beat me, too.

But wait a minute. What if we *all* went? They could not arrest everybody.

So after discussing it for a while, a group of seventeen people, including four of my own children, headed for Mendenhall City Hall.

We were met in the parking lot by Mark Sherman, the chief of police. Sherman was doing his best to defuse the situation. He promised us that Garland was being treated decently, that no one had "laid a hand on him."

"But you beat up Roy Berry," someone said.

Sherman had a quick answer for that one. His department had had nothing to do with Berry's arrest. That was handled by the county sheriff's department, so we needed to go over to the county jail if we wanted to find out anything about that case.

We decided that was exactly what we would do.

"We've come to see Roy Berry," I told the jailer as we crowded into his front entrance hall.

About a dozen of us followed him as he walked out of the lobby and into the booking room.

"We want to see Roy Berry," I repeated.

The jailer's response was surprising.

"You're all under arrest," he said.

Then he opened the big steel doors to the holding cell. Doug was standing just in front of me, so the jailer grabbed him and shoved him inside the cell. I followed right behind Doug, with everyone else right behind me. Surely they would not arrest all of us. But as soon as all twelve of us were inside the cell, the jailer slammed the big door shut and told us again, "You're all under arrest."

"What are you charging us with?" someone wanted to know.

"We just came here to see our friend."

"I can't breathe!" someone yelled.

"I'm going to smother!" another voice rang out.

The jailer did not know how to handle this situation, so he called for reinforcements. In a few minutes the sheriff had arrived, along with the district attorney and several officers from the Mississippi Highway Patrol. The Highway Patrol's primary purpose at this time in Mississippi's history seemed to be to help keep blacks in line, so patrolmen were always the white community's first line of defense against "belligerent" blacks.

These reinforcements stood off in a corner whispering with the jailer, trying to figure out what they were going to do with all of us.

Meanwhile, news of our lockup spread throughout the black community of Mendenhall (thanks to the five who had not followed the jailer into the booking room and had not gotten arrested), and our friends and families began gathering in the street outside the jail demanding to know what was going on. From the small cell window I could see Vera Mae in the crowd below.

Meanwhile, a big, mean-looking patrolman came over to the cell door. He was trying to be authoritative and polite at the same time.

"Tell you what, kids. If you leave nice and easy, nobody will be hurt. We just want to keep Reverend Perkins and this Huemmer fella overnight. But you kids better get out of here."

They were not buying it. One of them, speaking for the group, replied that if I was not allowed to leave, they were not leaving either. The other teenagers quickly added their agreement.

The officer shook his head, cursed under his breath and went back for another private discussion with the jailer and the others.

By this time the crowd in the street below had grown to well over a hundred people. We could hear their angry voices as they demanded to know what was going on in the jail. I could also hear the voice of someone calling out for the crowd to disperse peacefully. This man was saying I was a "false leader" who had gotten my people into all sorts of trouble, and that they ought to turn against me.

The speaker was a Highway Patrolman named Lloyd Jones. His nickname was "Goon," and he was proud of it.

The people were not buying what Jones had to say. Nor were they leaving without us. But the authorities were not about to release us.

I was grateful for the support of my friends and neighbors, but worried because I knew this standoff might erupt into violence at any moment. I was afraid for these kids in the cell with me. And I was afraid for their families and friends outside.

But I felt an emotion stronger than fear churning in my breast. It was a sense of overwhelming love for the people outside who had come here to stand with me against injustice. They really were my brothers and sisters, and I loved them so much at that moment that I could hardly contain it. I had to let them know how I felt.

I made my way over to the small window and, holding onto the bars from that second-story window, I began to call out to the people below.

I do not remember exactly everything I said that night, but I started off by telling them how much I loved and appreciated them. (When I said this, they cheered.) Then I warned them to be careful.

"I know how you feel," I called out. "I know you're angry. I know you feel like giving back what we've been getting all these years. But we can't do that."

If we resorted to violence to get our way, I told them, we would be lowering ourselves and getting down on the same level with the white thugs who loved to terrorize and brutalize us.

"If we give back hate for hate, anger for anger and violence for violence, we will lose what little we have already gained. And we'll have very little hope of ever gaining anything else."

There was total silence from the small crowd below. The people seemed to be listening intently to every word I was saying, and the words just poured out of me. I almost felt as if it was not me talking, but someone talking through me—and I knew God's Holy Spirit was helping me find the words that needed to be said.

After urging the people not to resort to violence, I added that it would be a terrible mistake if we simply caved in and did what the authorities wanted us to do—which was simply to go on back home and pretend that none of this had happened. There was a time when people had to take a stand against injustice, and that time, for us, was now.

"If someone has to suffer," I said, "I'm willing for it to be me. I'm willing to die if that's what has to happen."

But, I told them, I really could not do anything on my own. Neither could any one of them. We had to stand together, shoulder to shoulder. That was the only way we could finally gain our freedom from oppression. After all, this was about more than the twelve of us locked in a jail cell on this night. It was about the fact that most of the streets in the black section of town were in terrible condition, many of them not even paved. It was about living in a town where the best jobs were off-limits to people with black skin. And it was about the city's failure to provide even the most basic services for Mendenhall's black residents, who made up nearly one-third of the population.

Suddenly I got an inspiration. There was something we could do to make the white residents of Mendenhall take notice. If we hit them where it hurt, they would surely take seriously our demands for fair treatment. And where would it hurt most? In the pocketbook, of course.

The time was right for an economic boycott, especially during the Christmas season, normally the busiest time of the year for merchants everywhere.

I told my audience that it would take drastic measures to get our message across, and that those drastic measures would involve some self-sacrifice. Then I explained my idea of an economic boycott.

"I know a lot of you have put things on layaway," I said. "Well, leave them there! In fact, do not buy anything at all in Mendenhall. If you have to do some Christmas shopping, that's fine. Just don't do it here."

I reminded them that we had been hurting for years and that it was about time to let the white merchants of our town know how that felt. Maybe if they hurt a little bit, they would know how we felt, and maybe they would decide that the time had come to see that everyone in town was treated fairly.

I was not sure if everyone in the crowd was sold on my idea. But I knew from the response that I had hit on something. There were shouts of "Amen!" and "Right on!" and some enthusiastic applause. Then I knew my idea would work—because if a man has to choose between hanging onto his prejudices and hanging onto his money, he will almost always choose to let his prejudices go.

About this time, the authorities decided they had had enough of my speech and enough of the standoff. The sheriff announced that Doug and I were under arrest and that everyone else was free to go. If they did not go on their own, they would be forced to go.

That little speech did not change the kids' minds. They were not about to leave voluntarily. So the cell doors were unlocked and the other ten "jailbirds" were carried out one by one, every one of them screaming, "No! No! I won't go!"

There was nothing they could do about it, though. Soon Doug and I were the only ones left in the cell.

I felt bad for Doug because he had already missed his flight to California and it might be hard for him to find space on another flight since we were at the peak of the holiday travel season. But he was not sweating it. He was standing up for what was right, and it was clear that that was what mattered most to him. I admired him for his attitude.

Sometime in the middle of the night, around two or three in the morning, Doug and I were officially charged with our "crime" and moved to another cell.

Outside the temperature had fallen into the low 30s and the protesters, deciding they had done everything they could possibly do, had drifted off, most of them headed for the relative warmth and comfort of their homes.

The cell was not warm. It was not comfortable; it was bare and drab, and I felt tired and alone. Outside, the Christmas decorations of the city of Mendenhall shivered and shook in the icy wind. Inside I shivered in the icy reality that some people hate other people for no other reason than the color of their skin.

I thought about Garland Wilks and Roy Berry. I hoped they were O.K. and breathed a quick prayer on their behalf. Then I settled down and tried to get some sleep.

It did not come easily. For a brief moment I was tempted to doubt God's call on my life. I had never considered that His call might involve time in jail, yet here I was. Then I remembered some of the great men of the Bible who had spent time in a jail cell—people like Joseph, Daniel, Peter and Paul. I would not equate myself with any of those great heroes of the faith. But I took comfort from the fact that I was in some very good company!

I would have received a great deal of comfort, had I known, from what was going on elsewhere in our town that night. Not everyone had gone home. A large group, including Vera Mae and our children, had gone over to the Voice of Calvary church building, where they had begun shaping up plans for the economic boycott I had suggested. They stayed there all night, making dozens of picket signs. By eight in the morning they were already in place on the uptown streets, urging shoppers to take their business elsewhere until the city of Mendenhall began treating its black residents fairly.

To be honest, I think we were all surprised by the effectiveness of the boycott. It was a big sacrifice for some to stay out of those downtown stores. Some had put all their Christmas presents on layaway—dresses, bikes, sporting goods, toys, you name it. Only one more payment to go and all that stuff would be ready for wrapping and placing under the tree. If most folks did not get those things out of layaway, they would not have any kind of Christmas at all. And, of course, they would lose all the money they had already paid. So many had a hard choice to make. If they joined the boycott, they would have some very disappointed children come Christmas morning.

But most people decided the sacrifice was worth it. During what should have been the busiest shopping time of the year, the streets of our town were almost empty. Not only were we staying away from the stores, but so were most of the town's white residents, who did not want to confront the protesters.

Naturally, the store owners got panicky. They wanted something done and figured the best place to begin was getting Doug and me out of jail. They began applying pressure on the sheriff to get us released as soon as possible.

Shortly after ten that very morning he came to our cell and asked, in the nicest way possible, why I did not just post bail and go on home to my family. He just hated to see me sitting in jail during the Christmas season. As for Doug, he knew the boy was anxious to get on home so he could spend the rest of the holidays with his family.

Strange. He had not been worried about any of those things last night. I knew he was up to something and was not about to play his game. I sensed that I had the upper hand, even if I was the one in jail. And quite frankly, I enjoyed it. I suggested that if the sheriff wanted Doug and me out of jail, he should simply drop the charges against us.

He would not hear of that, because it would mean admitting that Doug and I had been locked up for no good reason. In other words, it would mean admitting the truth, and that just was not acceptable. So Doug and I said we would have to think about things for a while.

We were content to sit in jail until the end of the day, and then we made bail, confident that we had been able to turn a difficult situation to our advantage. Garland Wilks and Roy Berry were released, too.

After a lot of prayer, it was decided that we should continue with the economic boycott. The last thing we wanted to do was hurt or antagonize anyone. But we felt we had suffered in silence for far too long. We prayed that God would use our effort to open the eyes of the white community to what life was like for those who lived on the "wrong" side of town.

Then we drew up a list of demands and presented them to city officials. We told them that we were continuing with our boycott until:

- All charges against me, Doug Huemmer and Roy Berry were dropped.
- Work was begun on paving the streets in the black section of town.
- Law enforcement officials began acting in accordance with the U.S. Constitution with regard to arrest-and-search procedures.
- A representative number of blacks were employed by Mendenhall businesses.
- All public facilities, including schools, were desegregated.

We did not think we were being the least bit unreasonable. We were only asking for the rights that the white residents of our town took for granted. So we were disappointed when Mendenhall officials told us flat-out that they would not even consider giving us what we wanted. They acted as if we had asked for all the gold in Fort Knox and then some.

We felt we had no choice, then, but to continue the boycott until they began to see that we were serious.

So we continued our protest through January and on into February. Every Saturday during that two-month period, we would parade through town to illustrate our grievances, beginning on the Voice of Calvary grounds and winding our way up Main Street, around the courthouse, then back to our starting point. All the way hundreds of voices chanted, "Do right, white man, do right!" And all the way we were watched by dozens of armed deputies, Highway Patrolmen and policemen—every one of them white, heavily armed and, judging by the looks on their faces, antagonistic.

We were careful not to provoke the situation. We certainly did not want violence. I have to admit that sometimes I felt afraid. But I knew—we all knew—that God was with us. He gave us the courage and strength to continue what we had started.

One of the most difficult things for me during this time was the reaction—rather, the lack of reaction—from the white Christians of Mendenhall. There was not a single suggestion that—well, maybe we did have a few valid points. What's more, many of the whites who taunted and jeered us as we marched were members in good standing of their churches, people who considered themselves Bible-believing Christians. Where was the love and compassion of Christ? Still, I had to believe that the love of Christ would prevail and that Christianity was stronger than racism.

At first, I think, the white community hoped that our boycott would simply run out of steam. But as the weeks went by, it became apparent that this was not going to happen. In fact, just the opposite was taking place. Those Saturday parades were getting bigger and bigger, as blacks from neighboring communities joined us, along with many students from Tougaloo College in Jackson.

When things did not seem to be dying down on their own, members of the white power structure tried another tactic. They offered a local black minister two thousand dollars to try to talk people out of joining the boycott. He took their money and did his best to stop what we were doing. But nobody much would listen to him. So as far as the merchants were concerned, it was a couple of thousand dollars down the drain.

I did not know that things were about to take an ominous turn. They had tried to buy us off and it had not worked. Now they were going to try to beat us into submission.

On Saturday, February 7, 1970, like every Saturday, we marched. And, like every Saturday, a group of students from Tougaloo College were on hand to assist with the protest.

The march itself went off without a hitch. As usual there were heavily armed law enforcement personnel all along the parade route. As usual there were dozens of white onlookers who called us names and made obscene gestures as we marched past them. Also as usual, there were several police photographers snapping pictures of all the marchers.

Still, we all felt pretty good after the march. There is something exciting and invigorating about being part of a group of people standing together for what they know is right. And there is a kind of fellowship, a strong bond, that comes about when people go through the furnace of adversity together.

We were especially feeling that bond on that day. We were also grateful to God for His might and power that gave us the courage to be strong in the face of all those guns and clubs. We had no illusions. We knew those policemen were there to "keep the peace," and that if violence did break out, none of those men in uniform would rush to *our* aid. Thanks be to God, we had not only been able to stand together and show the white community that we were serious about our list of demands, but He had stayed the hand of violent men. There had been no real trouble associated with our protest.

So the afternoon of February 7 found some of us back at the church building on Voice of Calvary's property. We talked about how the day had gone, thanked and praised God for the help He had given us and made plans to get back together again the following Saturday.

The meeting broke up late in the afternoon, after which I thanked the college students for coming, told them good-bye and went home to put the finishing touches on my Sunday morning sermon.

It was about 7:30 P.M. when the phone rang. It was Louise Fox, telling me through her tears that the Highway Patrol had stopped Doug Huemmer's Volkswagen bus and that he and the nineteen college students with him had been arrested and taken to the Brandon jail.

Almost immediately Vera Mae knew something was wrong.

"What is it?" she demanded as soon as I hung up.

"It's the college students," I told her. "They've been stopped by the Highway Patrol."

"Well?" she encouraged me to continue. She was hoping to hear that they had been given a ticket for speeding or something simple like that, even though she knew better.

"All the kids who were with Doug have been arrested, and they've taken them to jail in Brandon."

"Brandon! Oh, no!"

Vera Mae and I both knew about Brandon. The sheriff there was a fellow by the name of Jonathan Edwards, a notorious racist best known for beating up blacks who had committed the "crime" of attempting to register to vote. Compared to the anti-black mentality that reigned in Brandon, our little town of Mendenhall was the capital of racial harmony and enlightenment.

It occurred to me that Edwards' son, Jonathan Edwards III, had been in Mendenhall that afternoon as one of the Highway Patrol's "official observers" of the march. He had been standing right next to Lloyd "Goon" Jones—the same Goon Jones who had been bad-mouthing me that night I spent in jail.

"So what are you going to do?" Vera Mae wanted to know.

I shrugged. "The only thing I know to do—go up there to see what's going on, try to get those kids out of jail."

She did not try to stop me. She knew I had to go. But she did not like it one bit.

"You be careful," was all she said.

Curry Brown and Joe Paul Buckley, friends of mine who were actively involved in the boycott, said they would go with me to Brandon, and I was not about to try to talk them out of it. I figured there was strength in numbers, and I also knew that I could use some company, some moral support, on the 45-minute drive. To be honest, I was half expecting that we would never make it to Brandon. There was probably a Highway Patrolman waiting and watching for us. We would be pulled over on some trumped-up charge and wind up spending the night in jail ourselves.

It never occurred to me that what had been planned for us was much worse than that.

I was starting to breathe a little more easily by the time we got to Brandon. The trip had been uneventful, although unnaturally quiet. The three of us were much too concerned about the events at hand to engage in small talk.

At the courthouse, a uniformed patrolman told us where to park. He seemed friendly enough and was almost gracious when we told him we wanted to see the sheriff.

"O.K. You stay here, and I'll go tell him you're here."

You know, he seemed almost too friendly.

We did not want to push the issue until we had to, so we did as he asked, standing quietly by our car, just waiting for the sheriff.

Only the sheriff never came.

Instead we were suddenly set upon by a dozen or more Highway Patrolmen. Jonathan Edwards III was there. So was Goon Jones. One of them told us we were under arrest while the others began searching our car and frisking us. How or why they thought we might be carrying weapons I will never know. We had never even hinted at violence, and they had to know that. I suppose that, being cowards, they just wanted to make sure we were not able to defend ourselves against them.

Once they finished searching us, they pushed us up the driveway toward the jail, treating us as if we were cattle headed for the slaughterhouse. They did not even wait until they got us inside before they started beating us, although Curry took the worst of it. One of the patrolman kicked him in the back and the side and punched him in the back of the head.

It was a nightmare, and it got worse once we were inside the jail. There were even more white men in uniform waiting there, all anxious to get their licks in. I honestly thought they were going to kill all three of us. Because of my faith in God, I was not afraid to die, although I certainly did not want to leave my family. And when I saw the hatred playing on those faces, I knew those men wanted us to suffer before they killed us. I did not want to suffer.

It is hard for me to think about what they did to us. When I look back to that time, it almost seems like a movie, as if it was not really me they were hitting and kicking. Only it *was* me, and I have the scars and recurring pain to remind me. I cannot believe that one man could treat another man so horribly for any reason, let alone because of the color of his skin.

Sheriff Edwards was in my face almost as soon as I was through the door, yelling about how I was a "smart nigger," but that I was not safe because I was not in Simpson County anymore. They knew how to treat "smart niggers" in Rankin County.

"This is a whole new ballgame, nigger! How do you like this, nigger?"

All the while he was yelling at me, he was hitting me with his fists. I had to fight my natural tendency to fight back, because I knew they would certainly shoot me if I did, the same way they had killed my brother Clyde so many years before.

I tried to put my hands up to protect myself from the blows, but they were coming from all sides as the sheriff's friends joined in the fun. These were big, strong men and they were punching the three of us as hard as they could. It hurt. It hurt terribly.

Finally I fell to the floor, half-unconscious, hoping that would make them stop. It did not. They just went to kicking me as hard as they could—in the side, the head, the groin, swearing and cursing at me all the while. Finally the darkness took me in.

But even that was not enough to stop them. They just waited until I began to come around, and then they started beating me again. I do not know how many times I drifted in and out of consciousness that night. I only know that the beating and kicking seemed to go on forever and that the pain was excruciating. I also remember that the first thing I would see, whenever I came to, was lots of blood all over the floor, and knowing that most of it—but not all of it—was mine. I knew I was not the only one being brutalized, and I wondered if they had killed anyone yet.

Not only were they beating me and Curry; they were also beating some of the college students. Sometime during the night they shaved Doug Huemmer's head and beard and poured moonshine whiskey all over him. Then they did the same thing to Curry. Because Joe Paul was older and had a heart condition, he was not subjected to such violence.

These men—men sworn to protect and serve the public—were having a party. All during the time they were beating us, they were walking among us drinking something (though I was beaten half out of my senses, I knew it was moonshine) out of paper cups. The more they drank, the more vicious they got, and that's saying something, because they were extremely vicious when the evening began. The more they drank, the more creative they got with their violence. I am quite sure it was the moonshine that gave them the idea of shaving Doug's head.

At some time during this long, terrible evening, they began to scream at me because I was bleeding on their floor.

"Hey, nigger," one of them said, "what are you doing bleeding all over my floor like this? Hey, Ralph, you see what this nigger done to our floor?"

"Why, that's disgusting," the other man replied, having hilarious fun at my expense. "You just get up right now and clean up this mess!"

Doug Huemmer was also beaten into unconsciousness several times during that night of terror, but he saw enough of what went on that he was able later to testify in court:

"Sheriff Edwards and Sheriff Edwards' son and two Highway Patrolmen that I do not know the names of and Officer Thames had a leather blackjack thing and they began beating on Reverend Brown, Reverend Perkins, David Nall and myself and one of the other students, and they beat Reverend Brown down to the floor, and then Reverend Perkins was dragged over on the other side and beaten down by about five other officers. I could hear him being beaten and . . . I heard them ordering Reverend Perkins to mop up the blood that was on the floor. . . . Reverend Perkins was lying sorta stunned on the floor and they kicked him until he got up. . . . Then Sheriff Edwards, Sheriff Edwards' son and two or three patrol officers would walk by every two or three minutes and kick or hit Reverend Perkins with one of their blackjacks or their feet."

They brought me a mop and bucket and forced me to start cleaning up the floor, even though I was so weak and in so much pain that I was afraid I would pass out at any moment. Then they continued to hit, slap and kick me because I was not doing a good enough job.

From what they were saying, I gathered that they thought some FBI agents were on their way to check out the situation at the Brandon jail. That is why they wanted the blood cleaned up, and why they ordered me, once the mopping was finished, to go into a back bathroom and get washed up. If they thought washing my face would hide the evidence of the horrible beating I had taken, they were wrong. Soap and water could not disguise the cuts, bruises or swelling.

Unfortunately, the FBI never showed up, which only made our captors even angrier than before. One of them came over to me and put a gun to my head.

"I think I'm gonna kill me a nigger!"

He pressed the cold steel hard against me, and I knew the end had come.

Slowly he squeezed the trigger.

Click. The chamber was empty. It was just another way for a man with a badge to have some fun.

They had a good laugh about it and then beat me into unconsciousness yet again.

By the time I regained consciousness, they had thought of another vicious game to play. Someone had brought in a list of the demands made by the black citizens of Mendenhall, and they thought it would be interesting to hear me read the demands out loud while they hit and kicked me for emphasis. By this time my head was hurting so badly I could barely see well enough to read, and my throat was so sore I could not speak much above a whisper.

"Nigger, read louder!" one of them demanded.

"I just hate a nigger who won't speak up," someone else snickered.

"Hey, nigger, I didn't quite get that demand of yours. Why don't you read it again so I'll know exactly what it is you want us white folks to do for you?"

I do not know how long this went on. I do not know how I lived through it. I had only one source of comfort—the fact that the Son of God Himself knew exactly what I was going through, because He had been treated the same way, and He was without sin. I tried my best to hang onto that thought, although I have to admit it was not always easy to do.

As I later testified, "They started torturing us. It was horrifying. I could not even imagine that this was happening. One of the officers took a fork that was bent down and he brought that fork up to me and he said, 'Have you seen this?' And he took that fork and put that fork into my nose. Then he took that fork and pushed it down my throat . . . and then they beat me to the floor."

Finally—I do not know why—they decided they had done enough for one night, and the beatings stopped. Maybe they were getting tired, or maybe they wanted to stop just short of killing us. But, mercifully, we were booked, fingerprinted and taken upstairs to our cells.

It is strange, I know, but lying in the cell with every part of my body hurting, I began to feel pity for the men who had beat me. I thought about what hate had done to them, turning them into brutal, unthinking savages. I thought about those faces twisted into unreasoning, snarling, hideous things, and I shivered.

I remembered how, the night I was in jail in Mendenhall, Goon Jones had been trying to stop rumors that we were being beaten inside the jail.

"Now really," he had said to Vera Mae, "do you think I'd do something like that?"

Vera Mae's reply had been, "Yes, I do."

Jones had pretended to be shocked and hurt by her answer. But tonight, stomping and kicking me with every bit of his strength, he had proven that she was right. Hate had done that to him.

I am sure that some of the guys who brutalized us so terribly thought of themselves as good family men. They loved their wives, were gentle to their children and good to their parents. But hate is a demon and it destroys men's souls.

I was determined that it would not destroy my soul. I did not want to be like those men. I did not want to hate back. In fact I knew that I could not hate those men. God's love would not let me hate anyone for any reason.

Sometime on Sunday morning, one of the guards came to my cell and told me I had a visitor. He led me into a little room where Vera Mae was sitting and waiting for me. Never have I been as happy to see anyone as I was to see Vera Mae that day.

I know she had to be shocked when she saw the condition I was in, but she did not let on. She could not afford to, because the jailer stayed right there with us, watching us and listening to everything we said.

Vera Mae put her arms around me and whispered, "What happened to you?"

All I could say was, "Get me out of here. They're gonna kill me first."

At that time there were 23 of us still in the Brandon jail, and it would take a lot of money to get us out on bond. But our friends rallied to our defense, many of them putting up their property to cover our bonds, and by three on Sunday afternoon I walked out of jail a free man.

But there were others left behind, and it was not until five the following afternoon that we finally raised enough money to get the last man, Curry Brown, out of jail. He was in horrible shape, and he had spent Sunday night listening to the taunts of the jailer, who told him that all his friends had forgotten him and that we had just left him to rot in jail.

As we had been released one by one, we had gone to the home of Luvell Purvis, a man who lived a short distance from the Brandon jail. Purvis was a quiet, dignified gentleman who did everything he could to treat our wounds and comfort us.

I was still resting there when Curry was brought into the house. At last we were all free. We wrapped our arms around each other, held each other and cried.

Later on, when doctors examined me, they found that the beatings I had sustained had done a lot of damage to my stomach, which led to surgery a year later.

It was hard when Vera Mae brought the children to the hospital to see me after that surgery. That was almost more than I could bear.

I remember specifically the reactions of two of my children when they saw me.

Derek, who was just a little guy, threw himself on the foot of my bed and sobbed, it hurt him so badly to see what they had done to his daddy.

Joanie, who was fourteen, just went stiff. She could not stand it and had to leave the room.

Vera Mae followed her outside and tried to comfort her, but Joanie did not want to be comforted. With tears in her eyes and anger in her voice, she told her mother, "I will never, ever like a white person again! I mean it. I hate them!"

Joanie was wrong. She was able to overcome her anger and mistrust of white people.

And it only took ten years.

45 Minutes to Live 7

Tom Tarrants

There was no warning. None at all. No mysterious sense of fore-boding. Nothing to make me think this mission was not going to be successful.

This was to be a Number Four—Sam Bowers' term for a mur-der. This time our aim was to do more than destroy a building. Meyer Davidson was going to get exactly what he deserved.

I had always known that secrecy is one of the keys to carrying out a successful terrorist attack. Until the mission is completed successfully, only those who have to know should know.

But that rule in this case had not been followed. Two brothers, Raymond and Wayne Roberts, had been informed in advance about what was going to happen, primarily because they were going to assist with the bombing. Both men had been active in the White Knights for some time and had proven their allegiance to the cause. Wayne, a nightclub bouncer with more muscles than brains, had been one of those convicted in the murders of the three civil rights workers in 1964. In fact, he was the trigger man. Strange to say it, but Wayne's seeming lack of intelligence made him seem like an unlikely traitor. He just did not have the brains to be an FBI informer.

If I had thought about things some more, I might have been at least a little suspicious of the Roberts brothers. After all, they had seemed almost over-anxious to have this bombing carried out.

Apparently, as I learned later, the FBI had broken them by threatening to kill them if they did not cooperate and offering to give them $80,000 in cash if they did. I should have known that those two boys' dedication to the cause would disappear at the first flash of big money. But I never suspected it. Hate often goes hand-in-hand with greed, and when it does, greed tends to be the stronger of the two impulses.

Thanks to help from Wayne and Raymond, then, the FBI and Meridian police knew exactly when and where I was going to strike. The only thing they did not know was that I would have a woman with me. They expected my partner to be Danny Joe Hawkins, a long-time member of the White Knights who had a penchant for violence. Instead I was teamed up with Kathy Ainsworth, a slim young elementary schoolteacher who, like me, had won the praise and approval of Sam Bowers.

Kathy and I reached Meridian about 11 P.M. and stopped at a fast-food stand so I could call Raymond Roberts. I told him, via the codes we used, to meet us at our prearranged rendezvous point, a truck stop a few miles east of town.

We did not have long to wait before Raymond got there. But when he did, he appeared agitated to see Kathy. I assured him that she was more than capable. It never occurred to me that he was upset by Kathy's presence because he was leading us into a trap, and knew that there was a good chance both of us would be killed. Despite Raymond's long involvement in terrorist acts, sending a young woman into a deadly trap was hard even for him.

Still, there was no way he could back out now. He finally agreed that he would go with us, as planned, to show us the Davidson house. After that, we would return him to the truck stop and go do the job.

When we got to the house, the streets were unusually quiet, without so much as the sound of a dog barking in the distance. It was dark. Everything seemed perfect.

We took Raymond back to the truck stop, then drove to a patch of woods north of Meridian on Highway 45, where I took the bomb—29 sticks of dynamite—out of the trunk of my Buick Electra, checked out the circuitry and set the timer for 2 A.M. This bomb consisted of an electrical detonator activated by a mercury switch and clock. I was not quite as comfortable with it as I usually was, but that was no big deal as far as I was concerned. A bomb, after all, was a bomb. I put it gingerly on the front seat between Kathy and me.

All that remained now was to make the drive back to the Davidson residence, plant the bomb and head off down the highway toward Miami. We figured to be safely in Florida by breakfast time, leaving the Meridian police and FBI to sift through the rubble that used to be Meyer Davidson's house.

It was nearly 12:45 A.M. by the time we pulled up in front of our intended target. Everything looked exactly as it had earlier, nothing out of place or suspicious-looking.

We parked a short distance from the house. I opened the door as quietly as possible and stepped out into the street, tucking my nine-millimeter Browning into my waistband as I did. It was comforting to have the gun, even though I was certain I would not have to use it. I reached back into the car, picked up the bomb— the exterior of which consisted primarily of a Clorox box—and walked around the front of the car and on into the Davidsons' yard.

I was about halfway up the driveway when the first shot rang out and someone shouted at me.

Oh, no! Davidson had seen us and was shooting at us from inside his house.

More shots!

No, these were not coming from the house. Someone had been waiting for us out there in the darkness, and whoever it was, there were several of them. Suddenly bullets were buzzing all around me.

I dropped the bomb and spun around, knowing that my only hope was to make it back to the car and get out of there. As I ran toward the car, my pistol fell from my trousers and clanked harmlessly onto the street.

I had to make it back to the car and the submachine gun that was hidden under the front seat. I did not have much of a chance, though; the gunfire grew intense. Somehow I managed to make it to the car, but not before taking a full load of buckshot in the upper right leg. The blast staggered me, but I had to keep going.

When I reached the car, Kathy helped me in.

Then almost instantly she exclaimed, "Tommy, I've been hit."

She had taken a rifle bullet at the base of her neck. I looked over and saw blood running down her shoulder.

"I've been hit, too," I told her. "But we're going to make it. Don't worry."

She didn't answer.

I managed to get the engine started, slammed the accelerator to the floor and took off down the street, even as more bullets blasted their way into the chassis of the car. When I looked again, Kathy was slumped over on the seat, half on the floor. Most likely she was already dead.

Meanwhile, a police cruiser was right behind us and one officer was hanging out the passenger window firing blast after blast from his shotgun. I was showered with glass as my rear window was blown out. They were right on my bumper.

My tires squealed as I turned a sharp right at the first intersection, then made another fast right. They stayed right behind me, still blasting away.

At the very next cross street I tried to shake them by turning left instead of right, but my tires had been hit, and blew out as I turned, causing me to skid out of control. I slid up over the curb and into the yard of the house on the corner. The cruiser had been so close behind that there was no way for it to avoid crashing into me, sending my car bouncing into a fire hydrant and slamming me up against the steering wheel.

Acting more from instinct than anything else, I grabbed the submachine gun from under the seat, jumped out of the car and emptied an entire clip in the direction of the cruiser. One of the policemen, the one with the shotgun, was hit and crumpled to the ground. The other officer dropped beneath the dash to get out of the way.

With my bullets gone, I dropped the gun and prepared to run. But before I could move, the other officer stood and blasted me with his shotgun. Buckshot stung my stomach and upper left leg.

I do not know how I did it, but I turned and ran, even though both legs were now full of buckshot and bleeding profusely. My momentary escape was made possible because the policeman who had shot me was more concerned with his wounded partner than he was with me. Instead of chasing after me to finish me off with another round from his shotgun, he was checking out his partner's injuries and radioing for help. I guess he knew that in my condition I would not get very far.

I ran into the backyard of a house nearby and made my way to the shrubs in the back. A chain-link fence behind the shrubs stood between me and freedom. If I could manage to climb the fence, I just might be able to get away. But I had chosen the wrong fence to climb. When I reached out for the top of the fence, a jolt of electricity surged into me and sent me sprawling into the bushes below.

I had already lost a lot of blood and could not make my body move. I had no choice but to lie there and wait.

I could feel myself drifting toward darkness. I was so tired, I just wanted to lie there and die. I knew there was no way out for me now. It would be better to die than spend the rest of my life in prison. And besides, I would go to heaven . . . or so I thought.

It did not take them long to find me. Sirens screamed in the night. I heard the sound of excited voices and saw the beams of police flashlights as they searched the ground nearby looking for me. Suddenly one of the lights shone in my face.

"There he is!" someone shouted.

Some men were walking toward me. I could not tell how many there were, but there were several—at least four. They kept their light trained on me as they came closer. I lay still, unable to move.

When the men were just a few feet away from me, they turned off the lights. I lay in complete darkness for only a moment, wondering what was going on.

Blam!

The deafening roar from a police shotgun was accompanied by excruciating pain in my right arm.

Blam! Blam! Blam!

Three more blasts followed in quick succession. Another bullet ripped into my arm, leaving it hanging by a thin section of bone and muscle. Two of the blasts missed me, but hit the ground close enough to my chest that bits of soil and grass were sprayed all over me.

I felt a stinging sensation as the second set of shotgun pellets tore into my arm, but nothing more in the way of pain. I was so close to death now, so numb, that it seemed little more than a dream.

Suddenly a light was shining straight down on me.

"Is he dead?" The question was asked with more than a hint of hopefulness.

"No," came the reply. "The son of a bitch is still alive."

"Shoot him! Shoot him!" The owner of the first voice was urging the owner of the second voice to finish me off.

"No! No!" a third voice chimed in. "Don't shoot! The neighbors are here!"

Just then an ambulance attendant ran up with a stretcher.

I would not be alive today if those neighbors had not come to see what was going on. My captors would have liked nothing better than to blow my head off right then and there, but they could not kill a wounded, defenseless man in front of a group of witnesses. Besides, it seemed unlikely that anything further was needed to finish me off. Death was obviously close at hand.

A few minutes later I was loaded onto a stretcher and placed into the back of an ambulance.

Nearby I heard someone say, "The woman is dead, and this one isn't going to make it."

For the first time I knew for certain that Kathy's wound had been fatal. But the numbness that had overtaken my body had also spread to my heart. I could not feel a thing, even when confronted with my own imminent death.

By the time we reached the hospital, physical sensation was beginning to return, and that was *not* good. Every beat of my heart sent pain pulsing throughout my body, and I begged them to give me a painkiller. They could not. I was so weak that the smallest dose of a sedative would have killed me.

I would gladly have taken any sort of an injection just to ease the pain, though. If it meant I was going to die, so what? I was going to die anyway. In fact, as I was being prepped for immediate surgery, one of the doctors said he did not think I could possibly survive for more than 45 minutes.

His statement was echoed by a stern-looking man in a police uniform who bent down to peer into my face. "The doctor says you're not going to make it." The voice and the face that went with it were devoid of compassion or concern. "You ought to talk while you can get it off your conscience."

What was it that American soldiers were allowed to disclose if they were captured—name, rank and serial number? They were not about to get any more than that from me. I was determined to be a good soldier, upholding the Klan's vows of secrecy to the very end.

Still, the voice persisted. What was Sam Bowers' role in the bombing? Was Danny Joe Hawkins involved?

I would tell them nothing.

The inquisition continued right up until the moment I was wheeled into the operating room. The I.V. in my arm was doing its job well and I felt myself being dragged down into the deepest darkness of sleep. I was told to start counting backwards from 100 . . . 99 . . . 98 . . . 97 . . . and that was it. I went out like a light.

What happened next in that operating room can be described only as a miracle. God spared my life.

I survived, although I had lost several pints of blood by the time I arrived at the hospital. I survived, although my right arm had been all but severed by the shotgun blasts, and a four-inch section of bone had been blown away.

At first surgeons thought there was no way to save my life. Dr. Hernando Aeril, who worked on me, told me later that I had no pulse or blood pressure when he first saw me. Later they thought there was no way to save my arm. Thankfully, they were wrong on both counts. I made it through the surgery and several hours in Intensive Care. As my condition improved, I was finally taken to a private room.

As I blinked my way back to consciousness the next day, there were a few moments when I could not figure out where I was. I had a terrible headache from the anesthesia, I was in pain from my wounds and I was disoriented. Then, with jarring suddenness, the whole nightmare came back to me.

Before I could be swept away by feelings of regret and despair, my mother, father and girlfriend were in the room with me, telling me they loved me, that they would stand by me and see to it that I got the best possible medical treatment. It was good to know they cared that much about me, that they were not going to turn away from me because of any embarrassment or pain I had caused them. They were with me as much as possible throughout my recuperation, which was long, slow and very painful.

All the while, armed guards kept watch inside and outside my room. I was an important person as far as the FBI was concerned. They were convinced that I knew enough to help them put Sam Bowers and the other leaders of the White Knights behind bars, thus effectively destroying the organization. The FBI figured I could assist them in other ways, too. By this time the Bureau had compiled a thick dossier on my background and knew I had been involved with other right-wing paramilitary groups, such as the Minutemen. If they could only get me to talk, they might bring down some other right-wing extremists.

I knew so much and was of such importance to the Klan, they figured, that my former colleagues would try to either rescue or assassinate me to keep me from talking. So there was always an armed guard or two posted nearby.

On one occasion, several weeks into my recovery, I was scheduled for further surgery on my arm. As I was wheeled down the hall to the operating room, I was surrounded by at least half a dozen policemen wielding shotguns or submachine guns. When we reached the operating room, several other officers, also heavily armed, were waiting to take over. That is how determined the authorities were to keep me alive and ready for my upcoming trial.

But despite what had happened to me, I still believed totally in the cause and was determined to fight the Communist/Jewish conspiracy to my last breath. There was no way I was going to talk.

Naturally, I had a lot of time on my hands as I lay in the hospital. I tried to read the New Testament, but just could not "get into it" and soon gave up. I spent most of my spare time rehashing the events leading up to the failed bombing, trying to figure out what had gone wrong. The more I thought about it, the more I was convinced that someone had informed on us. There was no other way the police could have been there waiting in ambush for us that night. We had always been careful to cover our tracks and avoid loose talk. But with all our precautions, the police had known exactly where we were going to be and when.

As I heard bits and pieces of conversation between the policemen who were guarding me, I became more convinced that someone in the White Knights had been an informer. But who? By the process of elimination, I figured it had to be the Roberts brothers. I did not want to think they would betray me, but it was the only answer that made any sense. They were traitors, and they had to answer for their treachery.

I thought about this quite a bit because I wanted revenge for Kathy's death and for the injuries I had suffered. But more than that, their actions had to be exposed and dealt with, because they had betrayed the cause.

A few days before I was scheduled to be released from the hospital, I had an unexpected visitor—a tall, strong-looking man with a mustache. He came over to my bed and extended his hand to me.

As we shook hands, I tried to remember if he was someone I knew.

"I'm Mike Hatcher," he said.

I recognized the name. Mike Hatcher was the police officer who had been on the receiving end of a burst from my submachine gun. He had been hit three times in the chest, including once in the heart. But, like me, he had lived. He was already up and around, seemingly very healthy.

It is hard to describe what went through my mind as I lay there and looked up into the face of a man I had almost killed. I did not know what to say, so I didn't say much of anything, just that I was glad to see he was doing O.K.

He stood there for an awkward moment or two. Then he said, "I just wanted to let you know that I'm a better man than you are."

He said it without the least bit of hostility or bitterness.

Then he left.

I am sure that Mike Hatcher came to see me partly out of curiosity. He wanted to get an up-close look at the man who had nearly killed him. But beyond that, I don't know. Maybe he knew I was just a young man and that there was still time for God to get hold of me and straighten out my life. He expressed that sentiment in a Christmas card he sent to my mother later that year—a card in which he wrote, "Only God can take care of His lost sheep."

How right he was.

But as for now, this lost sheep was well enough to be transferred to the Lauderdale County Jail to await trial on a number of charges, including attempted murder and aggravated assault on a police officer.

I will never forget my first day in the cell. Up until now I had done my best to keep an air of bravado about me, refusing to show even the slightest bit of emotion. But as I was ushered into a tiny cell and the heavy steel doors were locked behind me, I was overcome by despair and began to cry. I have never felt more alone or more hopeless as I did when I looked around that dingy, drab, dimly lit cell. My life was gone as surely as if I had died on that operating table.

Over the next four months, while I was awaiting trial, that cell was my home, and I never got used to it. The first few days were especially difficult, and if I had had any way to do it, I probably would have taken my life. I was so depressed that I slept most of the time, and I looked forward with great anticipation to Sundays and Wednesdays, because those were visiting days. Nearly every one of those days, my parents (who had divorced, though they later remarried) made the drive from Mobile—a roundtrip of nearly three hundred miles—to see me.

That was a great example of parental love, especially because they did not get much in return. I was depressed, moody and so consumed with my plight that I did not let them know how much I looked forward to their visits or how much I appreciated everything they brought me—things like newspapers, magazines and snack foods. I do not think I spent a single moment worrying about what my folks were going through. Part of my brutish behavior was brought on by selfishness, and part of it by my continued obsession with radical politics. I wanted to be out there on the front lines, not lying here in a jail cell reading *Time* magazine and eating Fig Newtons while a worldwide conspiracy was chipping away at our freedom.

I had some other visitors in the weeks leading up to my trial: two FBI agents named Frank Watts and Jack Rucker. Naturally I was not fond of the FBI. My feeling was that they should be going after the Communists, Jews and blacks who were trying to overthrow this country, instead of spending their time harassing patriotic Americans like me.

But as much as I detested the FBI, I found myself liking Rucker and Watts. Almost against my will, I looked forward to further visits. Their purpose in coming was to get information to help them break up the White Knights. But even though I was not about to give them what they were after, they seemed to take an interest in me—especially Watts. It is hard to see why he liked me, since I was not very likable at that time in my life, but he did.

Somehow, in the course of our conversations, the talk turned to spiritual matters. Watts was a Baptist, a churchgoing man. He could see that my understanding of the Scriptures was perverted— that I was using them to justify all sorts of anger, hatred and violence. He even asked his pastor, Dr. Bev Tenin of First Baptist Church of Meridian, to come to the jail and talk to me, which he did.

Unfortunately, I was absolutely convinced I was right and did not want to hear anything Dr. Tenin had to say. I was amazed that a man of such obvious intelligence could have been so deceived by the international conspirators. Instead of appreciating the pastor's concern for my soul, I was only irritated by it, the way I was irritated by my mother's occasional tears. I wanted her and my father to be as passionate about things as I was, but they did not understand what was going on in the world, though they gave me as much support as they could.

Along with all the other things my parents did for me, they retained two attorneys to represent me. I did not appreciate this either, especially when one of the attorneys, Thomas Haas, a former assistant U.S. attorney from Mobile, decided that my only chance to get off without serving time in prison was to plead innocent by reason of insanity. I did not like Haas in the first place. I thought he was far too liberal on civil rights and race issues, and was infuriated when he suggested the insanity defense.

Haas was sincere in his suggestion; he truly believed that anyone who acted the way I did had to be insane. (From today's vantage point, I would have to say that he was right. I had become so obsessed with right-wing radicalism that I had lost the ability to think objectively.)

Despite my objections and my insistence that he be fired, Haas went ahead with the insanity defense, and even sent a highly respected psychiatrist, Dr. Claude Brown, to talk to me while I was awaiting trial. During the trial Dr. Brown testified that, based on his evaluation, I should be given psychiatric treatment instead of being sent to prison. His testimony was backed up by my mother, who told the court about the drastic changes in my behavior that had taken place over the past few years.

It did not work. The prosecutor called the head of the state psychiatric hospital to testify as a rebuttal witness. He shot down Dr. Brown's testimony in short order.

It took the jury less than an hour to find me guilty as charged.

I was sentenced to thirty years in prison.

On December 13, 1968, I was transferred from jail in Meridian to the Mississippi State Prison at Parchman. For nearly six hours I sat in the back seat of a station wagon, shackled by handcuffs and chains, and watched the bleak winter landscape roll by. In spring and summer, the rolling hills of the Mississippi countryside are beautifully lush and green, but by mid-December all the colors have fled. The trees stand bare and brown against a pale gray sky, most of the grasses have turned yellow and brown, and the cotton stalks are brown and empty.

But the bleak countryside was nothing compared to the bleak landscape of my soul. Every time I thought I had sunk as far into depression as I could go, something else happened to prove me wrong. I could not cry anymore; I was so empty that tears would not come.

Sharing the station wagon with me were five other prisoners, two white and three black. I had no idea what the other men's offenses were, but I knew that, because of the violent nature of my own crime, and because of my ties to the White Knights, I was an MIP—a Most Important Prisoner—and that meant we got special attention. We were escorted all the way to the prison by two Highway Patrol cars, one in front and the other in back, and at various checkpoints along the route other vehicles joined us. We never went much slower than 80 miles per hour. They were doing everything they could to make an ambush impossible, just in case anyone had ideas of setting me free.

At the prison I was separated from my companions and taken to the maximum security area—a place notorious for its harsh conditions and brutality. Here I would be sharing life with the worst sorts of criminals, including murderers, rapists and bank robbers. It was not fair. I was no criminal; I was a revolutionary, a prisoner of war.

But the Mississippi State Prison did not have a special section for revolutionaries or prisoners of war. So there I was with a guy who had shot and killed his best friend in an argument over three dollars, another guy who had stabbed his girlfriend because he had not liked the way she cooked dinner, and a bunch of people who thought that sort of thing constituted normal behavior.

Actually, my cell was on death row, although only five of the many prisoners here had actually been given death sentences. This was a dank, dark place where men lived in small concrete cubicles behind steel bars. As a new resident here, on December 20 I "celebrated" my twenty-second birthday.

Sometimes prisoners with behavior problems were sent here for attitude adjustment. They might be placed in a room known as "the black hole," a small cell that was completely enclosed and thus completely dark when the door was closed. Or sometimes during the summer the exhaust fans might be turned off, which usually got prisoners' attention in a hurry. Another extreme form of discipline was to ply an especially unruly prisoner with heavy laxatives, then handcuff him to the bars on his cell door.

Bad behavior was not taken lightly.

There was not much variety to life on death row. Basically we sat in our cells hour after hour, day after day. We were let out only twice a week for thirty minutes to shower and shave.

A few days before Christmas, a riot broke out. I did not know what caused it, but prisoners set their mattresses on fire and broke up their commodes. I was one of only three prisoners in the entire cellblock who did not take part. The reason I did not take part, frankly, was that I thought the whole thing was stupid. There was nothing at all to gain from it.

When the sergeant in charge of the maximum security unit came to inspect the damage, he was surprised that my cell was as neat and orderly as usual, with my bed made and nothing out of place.

More or less as a reward for our refusal to get involved in the riot, the warden transferred me and two other prisoners to the hospital unit, where we were given jobs. Mine was as a laboratory technician trainee.

Living conditions were much better there. I shared a small dormitory room with several other men. We had our own television set, a bathroom with a door that closed and (at least, comparatively speaking) good food to eat.

While I was working in the hospital, I became good friends with the prison physician, a black doctor named Luther McCaskill. McCaskill, who was in his mid-thirties, was serving time for performing an illegal abortion on a woman who later died from complications. He was a genuinely compassionate man, someone who always tried to see things in the best possible light. His conviction had cost him his career, but he did not seem bitter or angry.

Dr. McCaskill knew all about my background, my extremist views on matters pertaining to race, and the fact that I was in prison because of violence associated with the Ku Klux Klan. But he did not seem to hold any of that against me. He treated me the same way he treated everyone else, respectfully and cordially, and I found myself liking him immensely, almost in spite of myself. Another thing that was obvious about Dr. McCaskill was that he was an intelligent man. It was hard to be a racist when I was spending so much time with a man like that.

Working with Dr. McCaskill, I was able to see the worst side of prison life. We were kept busy tending to sick and wounded prisoners. The ones who came to us most often had been injured by other prisoners. There were numerous stabbings, beatings and even shootings.

On one occasion the prison cook and baker were brought in, both in critical condition and both spurting blood. These men had been drinking, become involved in an argument and fought it out with butcher knives. The cook's arm had been all but severed. Tendons, muscles and bones were exposed and his arm hung by a thread. The baker had several deep stab wounds in his chest and was near death from loss of blood. Fortunately, Dr. McCaskill was able to save the lives of both, though it was quite a while before either one of them recovered completely from his injuries.

Some of the wounds we saw came as the result of homosexual behavior. Homosexuality was a problem at the prison, and some men were beaten because they would not submit to the advances made by stronger men. Jealousy also provoked numerous vicious fights among prisoners.

All in all, even though the prison hospital was a much better place to be than death row, it was still horrible and I wanted out. It did not take me long to make up my mind that I would try to escape. As far as I was concerned, there were only two questions: How would I get out and when would I do it?

The more I analyzed the situation, the more convinced I became that I would never be able to escape on my own. I needed to find some men who wanted out as badly as I did, men who were intelligent and trustworthy. I began assessing every prisoner I knew, asking myself if he would make a good accomplice.

The first likely candidate was not hard to find. Louis Shadoan worked as a clerk in the I.D. office. He was serving a long sentence for bank robbery and talked proudly about every bank he had robbed. I wondered how Louis had ever been caught since he was an extremely intelligent man (prison officials had measured his

IQ at 160) and he seemed like the type who must have planned each job very carefully.

Because Louis worked in the prison I.D. office, it was fairly easy to find an opportunity to spend some time alone with him. I did not know how he would react and was relieved to find out he was glad for my asking about his interest. He thought it was a great idea, and of course he would go with me.

Over the next few weeks, Louis and I kept careful watch of everything that went on in our areas of the prison. We paid especially close attention to the daily operation of the hospital unit, noting details like when and how supplies were delivered, when garbage was picked up and what time the changing of the guard occurred.

We finally decided that the best time to make our escape would be early evening, just after dark, when there was only one civilian guard on duty in our compound. If we played it right, it would be fairly simple to overpower him. The guards who kept watch in the prison tower at night were trustees—inmates who had been given special freedoms and responsibilities within the penitentiary—so we figured it would be a simple matter to bribe them. Once we were past those guards, we would need a safe place to hide out for a time until we could arrange for transportation to wherever it was we decided to go.

To help us with that phase of the operation, I was able to obtain a map of the entire 16,000-acre prison farm, complete with all the surrounding roadways. Louis and I also began drawing up a list of the supplies we would need on the outside, including food, medical supplies, clothing, arms and ammunition.

During this time I was smuggling letters out of the prison to two of my friends in the White Knights. I told them of our plans to escape, and they sent back word that they would assist us in any way they could. They began stockpiling the supplies we needed and began making visits to the Parchman area to locate the best possible rendezvous points at which to meet us escapees.

As the time approached, I got more and more excited about returning to the free world. Our escape plans were well conceived. Our chances of failing were low. But the more we talked about our plans, the clearer it became that we needed to bring in a third person. Another man would increase our strength in a number of ways. He would make it easier for us to overpower whatever guards might try to stop us. And we could certainly use an extra set of eyes.

We finally decided to talk to Malcolm Houston, a young man in his twenties who had tried once to escape but failed. In spite of his previous failure, we considered him a reliable man.

For his part, Houston was more than receptive to making another escape attempt.

Shortly after we included him in our plans, I received word from my two friends on the outside that they had been able to gather the supplies we needed and had found a safe place for us to use as a hideout for a few days. All that remained was for us to pick the day of our escape.

After checking the calendar, we decided that July 23, 1969, would be ideal. Our final challenge was to find a way to confirm plans with our pickup on the day of the escape. Specifically, we needed a method whereby our outside helpers could let us know that they would definitely be at the rendezvous point waiting for us. We also agreed that if something prevented us from getting out of prison on the first night, our accomplices would be waiting at the rendezvous point on the next night, too, and even a third night, if necessary. After all, it was possible that something unexpected would happen on the 23rd that would force us to change our plans, and maybe on the 24th, too. But we felt sure we could do it one of those days.

Confirming our plans on the day of the escape would not be easy. It was not possible to make phone calls in or out of the prison. Letters were too slow. We finally hit on the idea of having the outsiders place a classified ad in the Jackson *Daily News,* an afternoon newspaper that was delivered to the prison. The ad would read:

Lost: German shepherd. Name Sam. Black and Silver in Color. Large Size.

If that ad did not appear in the paper on the 23rd, then we would postpone the escape. If it did appear in the paper, it was a signal that all systems were go.

July 23 was one of the longest days of my life. I was tense and excited, and found it a real struggle not to let my emotions show. Several times during the day, my prison job took me to Louis' and Malcolm's offices. I knew they were every bit as nervous as I was, but they were playing it very low-key.

The newspaper usually arrived about five in the afternoon, but today for some reason it was late. By this time, tension was building in me to the point that I thought I was going to explode—and I found myself thinking that that ad had better be in the newspaper that afternoon.

5:15 and still no paper. 5:20 and it had not come. It was never this late. What if it did not come at all? Had prison officials found out what we were up to somehow and confiscated the newspapers? Could people tell how nervous and tense I was? Would they know I was up to something?

Finally, about 5:30, a trusty arrived with the few copies of the paper that came to the prison hospital.

Louis got one of the papers, tucked it under his arm and came by my office. I was almost afraid to look.

But there it was. Someone had lost a German shepherd named Sam. There at the bottom of the ad was a friend's phone number. Tonight was the night.

With help from the head cook, Louis went to the prison kitchen and stole three large butcher knives—one for himself, one for me and one for Malcolm. We concealed the knives in our clothing. We were almost home free.

We offered no resistance when the time came for us to be locked in our dorms for the night—Malcolm and me in one dorm, Louis in another. We knew that the night watchman and his trusty would be coming around shortly before eight o'clock to give medicine to the prisoners who needed it, and we would be waiting for them.

They came right on schedule and Malcolm and I grabbed them, flashed our knives and told them we would kill them if they did not cooperate. They were not about to argue when faced with those huge blades. They told us they would do anything we wanted if we would just not hurt them.

Next, with the night watchman's keys, we went across the hall and let Louis out of his dormitory. Everything was going exactly according to plan.

We tied up the night watchman and trusty with adhesive tape we had stolen from the prison emergency room. Then we went to the front hall of the hospital, where the night watchman's desk and intercom system were located. First we called our friend who was on duty in the guard tower. He had already been informed that this was the night of our escape, so he came in and allowed us to wrap him up with the adhesive tape.

Once that had been done, we called in the only other guard, who was on duty in front of our compound. This was risky. He might sense that something was up and summon guards from other areas of the prison. Fortunately for us, he did not suspect anything and came down to see why he was needed. As he came into the room, Louis hit him over the head from behind, knocking him to the floor. Before he could regain his balance, Malcolm and I were on him, flashing our knives and letting him know not to resist. He was soon tied up just like the others.

All that was left was for us to walk outside, get into the night watchman's car and drive off.

Our plan was to drive down to an irrigation creek that ran through the prison. We knew that a bridge over the creek had been washed away, and we were going to leave the car there. We wanted to make it look as though we had not known about the washed-out bridge, that we had been forced to abandon our car and that we were probably somewhere in the vicinity on foot. Actually, the irrigation creek was only about a mile from our chosen rendezvous point. We would meet our accomplices there and be well on our way down Highway 49 while searchers were still combing through the cotton fields around the prison.

We had no idea how tough that final mile was going to be! The first thing we had to do was wade across the creek, a distance of perhaps thirty feet. What we had not counted on was that the bottom of the creek-bed was soft, gooey mud several inches thick.

Every time you took a step, you sank down nearly to your ankles. Add to that the fact that we were moving through waist-high water flowing at a fairly good rate of speed, and it is no wonder it took us a long time to get across.

It was probably no more than five or ten minutes, but it seemed like hours because we knew it would not be long until our escape was discovered (if it had not been discovered already) and the guards would be on our trail. There had been numerous escape attempts from the Parchman prison, and most of the escapees had not gotten very far. The authorities knew every square mile of this country and they had bloodhounds to help them.

But finally we crossed the creek and were running through Mississippi cotton fields, heading as fast as we could, our water-logged shoes squishing with every step, toward our rendezvous point.

It was none too fast. For one thing, it had been a terribly hot, muggy Delta day, and even though darkness was setting in, the temperature had not fallen much. For another thing, we had not been able to get much exercise while we were locked in prison, and we were out of shape. We were gasping for breath and sweating profusely before we had run more than a couple of hundred yards. By the time we had run a quarter of a mile or so, my legs were about to give out, my stomach was cramping and my heart was beating so loud and hard I thought it was about to jump out of my chest.

Yet I was obviously in better shape than Louis and Malcolm. They were far behind me. I stopped and turned to wait for them. It almost looked as if they were running in slow motion.

"Come on, we're almost there!" I yelled.

There was no reply from my companions except their heavy breathing—wheezing, really.

Somehow we all kept running. The wooded thicket was just ahead.

"There it is!" I encouraged them. "We've made it! We're free!"

There was only one problem. I did not see my friends anywhere. Had there been some mistake? Had they become frightened and left the area?

Twice I called out their names. There was no answer.

Then we heard a welcome sound. A car engine started up and a gray Buick Electra convertible appeared from somewhere out of the darkness and screeched to a stop in front of us.

"Get in! Get in!"

My two friends seemed to be in a terrible hurry, and as we piled into their car, we found out why. They had been monitoring prison and state police radio transmissions, and told us that our escape had been the main topic of conversation for at least the last ten minutes. A search had already begun, and the authorities were in the process of sealing off the prison grounds. We had to move as fast as possible if we were to have any chance of getting away.

My friends had guns for all of us: pistols for Louis and Malcolm and an AR-15 automatic rifle for me. They also had a sackful of hand grenades. No doubt about it, they had come prepared for battle.

On the radio we heard that the night watchman's car had been discovered. They assumed, as we had hoped, that our escape had been thwarted by the washed-out bridge and that we were still somewhere in the immediate area on foot. That meant they would concentrate their search there. That made us all feel better. Still, we were a long way from our planned hideout, and longer still from our final destinations.

At one point, while we were still traveling on dirt roads not far from the prison, we were surprised by a pair of headlights that appeared suddenly in our rear-view mirror. It was immediately apparent that those lights were gaining on us fast. There was no doubt in any of our minds that it was a prison vehicle. If it caught up with us, we would certainly be pulled over so they could check us out.

Our driver was not about to let that happen. He slammed the gas pedal to the floor and we shot off into the night. Within a few minutes we could no longer see headlights behind us. The other vehicle had been unable to keep up with us, probably because we had stirred up so much dust he could not see where he was going.

It seemed forever, but we finally left the prison miles behind us and, by continuing to monitor police frequencies, managed to avoid roadblocks that had been set up along the main highways. It was about two in the morning when we reached our hideout— an old abandoned house and barn in a heavily wooded area about two miles from the Jackson airport.

We decided to set up headquarters in the barn, since it was the farthest building from the road that fronted the property. As soon as we unloaded our things, our two accomplices left, explaining that they would return the following night with more supplies, including food.

The rest of the night Louis, Malcolm and I took turns standing guard and sleeping. By daybreak we were all feeling pretty good. If the authorities had not found us by now, they probably were not going to.

That day passed without event. We continued to take turns standing guard, and I scouted the area as much as possible to give us a better understanding of the lay of the land. We also spent time talking about what we were going to do with our new-found freedom. Louis wanted to go to California. Malcolm was bound for New Orleans. I was going back into the bombing business, continuing my fight against the international conspiracy. But first I would go to South America to link up with some old Nazis and hide out for a while.

That night, true to their word, our accomplices returned with supplies and several bags full of groceries. For some reason, though, one of the men decided to bring along his fiancée. I could not believe he could be so stupid, and I told him so. Only five people should know where we were: Malcolm, Louis, the two outside accomplices and myself. Bringing any more people into the situation was inexcusable.

He was indignant. He swore that his fiancée was completely trustworthy and that he would not have brought her here if he thought there was even a remote chance she would give us away. I still was not convinced, but there was nothing I could do about it. The damage had been done.

Still, that night and most of the next day passed uneventfully. We continued to take turns standing guard and were happy to see that news broadcasts had less and less to say about our escape. From what we could tell, the authorities were baffled. Nevertheless, we took the extra precaution that day of moving out of the barn and into a tent we had set up in some heavy brush nearby. The reason for this was to eliminate the possibility of a surprise attack trapping us in the barn.

It was my turn to stand guard in the late afternoon. It was the hottest part of a terribly hot and humid day, and I was miserable. I had not been able to get more than six or seven hours of sleep in the two days since our escape, and I was dragging. Louis was due to relieve me around 7:00 P.M., and I was delighted when I saw him coming toward me a good thirty minutes early.

"It's too hot to sleep," he told me, explaining why he had come early.

I told him it was not too hot for *me* too sleep. And I was right. Back in the tent, it was no more than five minutes before I was dreaming away.

But I had not been out for more than a few minutes when I was awakened by several loud bursts in quick succession. I sat up, unsure if I had really heard something or if I was having a vivid dream. Malcolm sat looking back at me with the same confused expression on his face.

More blasts.

There could be no doubt this time. We were hearing gunfire, and it was coming from the area where Louis was standing guard.

Before we had a chance to react, a police helicopter was hovering overhead.

They had found us.

There were no further sounds of gunfire. Instead, a voice speaking over a bullhorn told us that Louis had been killed and that we were surrounded. We were ordered to surrender.

We had no choice but to obey, so we walked out with our hands held high in the air. Immediately we were surrounded by about twenty lawmen, FBI agents and members of the state police, who ordered us to take off our clothes and lie down on the ground. Then they searched us thoroughly.

Once they were convinced we were unarmed, they allowed us to put our clothes back on. Then they tied our hands behind our backs and loaded us into a car for the trip back to prison.

I felt terrible that Louis was dead. And I realized that if he had not come to relieve me early, I would have been the one killed. But the way I felt, going back to a tiny, dark prison cell, I almost wished I *had* been the one to die.

A Conversion of Love

John Perkins

It took me a long time to recover from the wounds I received in the Brandon County Jail. Actually I have not fully recovered to this day, even though it has been nearly a quarter of a century. I still have aches and pains related to the beating I took, and my stomach has hurt me ever since that night. I have been hospitalized for ulcers and have had to have a large portion of my stomach removed.

So the reminders are always there.

But they are reminders to me not of the hatred of men but of the love of God. When I am hurting, it brings to my mind the pain Jesus Christ took upon Himself on my behalf. I was beaten. Well, so was He. I was cursed and spat on by men who had no reason to hate me . . . and He was, too. Even as they were killing Him, He prayed, "Father, forgive them, for they know not what they do." And because Jesus is my example, the One I want to pattern my life after, I had no choice but to forgive the men who beat and tortured me. I have to admit, though, there were times when that was not such an easy thing to do.

Just about a year after the beating incident, I was hospitalized for several weeks after a severe attack of ulcers. Being laid up like

129

that gave me plenty of time to think about things—to evaluate where I was headed with my ministry. The first few days I could not help but think about all the ways white people had tried to stop anyone fighting for justice for the black citizens of Mississippi. I thought about that night in Brandon, of course, because I knew that the beating had caused my health problems. But I thought about a lot of other things, too.

I thought about the Klansmen who had threatened us with unsigned notes sent through the mail and anonymous telephone calls during the very early hours of the morning. I contemplated the "proper" businessmen who may not have been in the Klan but who still would not give us an even break. And then I spent some time thinking about those white men with uniforms and badges who tried to disguise their hatred and brutality as "law and order."

As I lay in that hospital, my mind also turned to the white churches of Mississippi. Many of those churches spent thousands of dollars every year to send missionaries to preach the Gospel in "darkest Africa" but would not allow a black American to enter their sanctuaries. A couple of friends of mine—one black and the other white—had attempted to attend one of the largest white congregations in the town of Mendenhall and had been asked (rather impolitely) to leave. They were told they were not welcome and to "get out of here right now," and it happened while the congregation was singing the Doxology: "Praise Him all creatures here below." Just not black creatures. Not in that church, anyway.

I also thought about some of the things my children had been through, especially the older ones, who had been the first blacks to attend their school in Mendenhall. Spencer, who was in high school, had told me how, when he was standing in line in the cafeteria, the other kids stood as far from him as possible and acted as if they were going to catch some terrible disease if they got too close. Then, as he went through the line, the server would give the white kids on either side of him big portions but make a point out of giving him a tiny piece, or a scrap or two from the side. In class, when the students were handing papers to one another, some of the white kids would get a kick out of acting as if anything Spencer had touched was contaminated. They would wrinkle their noses, make faces and carry on as if it might kill them to touch anything he had touched. Do you think the teachers did anything to stop that kind of behavior? Of course not.

Sometimes Spencer went with some of his friends to a swimming hole just outside of town. White kids would come down there with their daddies' rifles and shoot just over their heads. Like father, like son. Some of those kids, including my children, could have been killed. It hurts when people do or say certain things to you, but it is even worse when they do or say them to your children.

But once again, as I thought about things in the hospital, it took my mind back to Christ, the only begotten Son of God.

Still, I was tempted strongly to believe that cooperation between blacks and whites was impossible—that America's white-controlled society would never be willing to share on an equal basis with those with black skin, or brown, or red, or yellow. When you have been mistreated by a group of people from a particular race, it is difficult to keep it in proper perspective. It gets to the point that you think that the people who have pushed you around are representative of the entire race. You have thoughts that "they're all like that."

It was easy for me to see, as I lay in that hospital bed thinking about it, why so many leaders of the civil rights movement were so vehemently anti-white. They had been bruised and battered and beaten to the point that they began to believe there was not a single spark of goodness in the entire white race.

Yes, those kinds of feelings are racist. Yes, they are wrong. I am not saying for a moment that anyone is justified in stereotyping an entire race of people; I am just saying that I understand how it can happen. Believe me, I understand.

But when my thoughts were tempted to turn in that direction, God brought other white faces to my mind: white doctors who had tended to me in a caring, compassionate way; white attorneys who were standing beside me as I battled the state of Mississippi; white college graduates who were working for Voice of Calvary Ministries and earning only $100 a month; white preachers who had begun to speak out against racism and call for racial reconciliation. I thought of white kids like Doug Huemmer and Ira Freshman, who had shared that night of terror in Brandon.

In Mississippi at that time, it seemed to me that these were only a few positives against an overwhelming backdrop of negatives. But they were positives nonetheless and, I hoped, an indication of things to come.

Stronger than all these images playing through my mind was another powerful, soul-stirring, body-shaking scene—and that was the image of the Son of God dying on the cross of Calvary. I saw Him bruised and battered, His back torn apart by the brutal whipping He had endured, His hands and feet pierced through with huge spikes and blood running down His face from a crown of thorns that had been pushed down onto His head by a blood-thirsty group of Roman soldiers. I saw Christ as He felt so alone and abandoned that He cried out, "My God! My God! Why have You forsaken Me?" Yet Christ looked at those who had treated Him cruelly and prayed, "Father, forgive them, for they know not what they do."

The Holy Spirit would not let that image leave me. He seemed to be whispering to me again and again, "John, you've got to love them."

"But I don't want to love them! Look what they've done to me."

There was that image of Christ: "Father, forgive them. . . . " I simply could not get it to leave me alone.

"How can I love them, Lord?"

"Let Me love them through you."

And that is exactly what happened. The love of God began to take from my soul every bit of anger and hatred. The only way I can describe it is to tell you that I was overwhelmed by the love of God. And as His love and joy coursed through my spirit and soul, I knew there was no way I could keep that love from over-flowing to the people around me. White people, black people, any other kind of people, it did not matter. God loved them all and so did I.

Evil is a strong force, and hate one of evil's best weapons. But love is, and always has been, stronger than hate. Good is stronger than evil. Light is more powerful than darkness. In the end, love will prevail.

I might go so far as to say that I experienced a second conversion while I lay in that hospital bed. It was a conversion of love and forgiveness. And I was more determined than ever to move ahead in the quest for justice, reconciliation and love.

Thank God Almighty, I'm Free at Last!

Tom Tarrants

I was back in Parchman Prison, back on death row again, and I was going to be here for a long time. The borders of my world would now coincide with the borders of this tiny six-by-nine-foot cell.

I was not going to be given another chance to make a break for freedom. They would keep me on the shortest possible leash. As before, I would be given no other privileges except to be let out of my cell twice a week for a quick shave and shower. I was alive but would spend my days locked in a concrete and steel tomb.

But as hard as it was, being confined to such a small space was not the worst thing about prison life.

For one thing, the heat was oppressive. This section of the prison had no air conditioning, just a ventilator fan that did not do much to cool things off. When the temperature hovered around 90 outside, as it did almost every day the first six weeks after my capture, I felt as if I were living in an oven. The cellblock would heat up almost unbearably during the day and was slow to cool off in the evening, resulting in many sleepless or near-sleepless nights.

Another big problem for me was the noise. It was constant and very loud. If you have ever lived in an apartment where the people upstairs liked to have noisy parties, you know how annoying that sort of thing can be. Well, despite my violent ways, I have always enjoyed quietness. But this cellblock was crowded with men who liked their music as loud as possible, and it seemed that every guy in there listened to a different radio station. This was not all. There were other guys screaming to carry on a conversation above the constant cacophony of all the radios. This made the noise every bit as unbearable as the heat. At one point a "noise war" broke out in which almost all the prisoners made as much noise as possible. This went on for two days and two nights until fatigue forced the "warriors" to call a truce. After that, the regular noise did not seem quite as bad as before.

A third problem I had to face was boredom. I began to read everything I could get my hands on. Much of it came from my parents, who still came to see me as often as possible, sometimes bringing my younger brother and sister with them. Whenever they came for a visit, they brought some books and magazines, although they still did not get much from me in return. Then they succeeded in getting me transferred to another, quieter cellblock where I could enjoy reading more.

They brought me news magazines like *Time* and *Newsweek* and novels like *Gone with the Wind*. I was also able to order books through the mail, and I took advantage of the opportunity to acquire a number of books that supported my extreme racism—my battle against the international conspiracy. I read *The Inequality of Human Races* by Count Arthur de Gobineau, *White America* by Ernest Cox and even *Mein Kampf* by Adolf Hitler. I was also a regular reader of *The Thunderbolt, The Fiery Cross* and the John Birch Society's *American Opinion* magazine.

One of the books that had a profound impact on me was *Imperium* by Ulic Varange. *Imperium* is a book of neo-fascist philosophy, but it was not the author's ideas that affected me as much as it was the great philosophers he quoted. It made me want to read them for myself, which is exactly what I decided to do. That was the first step on a journey that would change my life.

The first book I read was Hegel's *Philosophy of History*, which I followed with Oswald Spengler's *Decline of the West*. I found both books intriguing, although there were some concepts that were hard to grasp. From that beginning I moved on to the works of Plato, Aristotle, Socrates and the Stoics. I was fascinated by the writings of these men—especially by Plato's determination to seek truth no matter what the cost, and Socrates' declaration that the unexamined life is not worth living.

As I read the works of these great thinkers, it came home to me that if I was really interested in truth, I would have to examine viewpoints that did not agree with mine. In order to know that my beliefs were correct, I would have to know what other people were saying. Until this time I had limited my reading to those books and magazines that reinforced the way I already felt. In that sense my life was "unexamined." I had closed myself to any other understanding of what was going on in the world. If an unexamined life is not worth living, it must also be true that an unexamined opinion is not worth holding.

So I began to read the works of authors who saw the world differently than I did. I did not think it would change anything. I was confident there would be obvious errors in logic and reasoning that would deflate the arguments of my opponents and leave me more secure than ever in my right-wing radicalism.

But as I read *Legacy of Freedom* by George C. Roche, I began to see the complexity of history—how many different factors influence world events. In this complicated and diverse world, I had been looking for a simple answer—a scapegoat for all the world's ills. That simple answer had been the international Jewish/Communist conspiracy, and the scapegoat had been the Jews and their "partners in crime"—the blacks.

I did not immediately see the fallacy of the views of the extreme right wing. Ideological thinking still controlled me. In a sense, right-wing radicalism was my identity. I had all but sacrificed my life in defense of these views, and it was not easy to admit, even for a moment, that they might be wrong. But many facts did not square with "the truth" I had believed for so long.

We had always made a big deal, for example, out of the fact that Karl Marx was a Jew. That was just another indication, we said, that Communism was nothing more than a Jewish plot to take over the world. I had never heard that when Marx was still a young boy, his father had converted to Christianity, and that Marx himself was an atheist who held Jews, and all others who believed in God, in contempt. Communism as a philosophy was vehemently anti-religious, and that included the Jewish religion. How then could it be part of an international Jewish conspiracy?

Gradually the wall of right-wing ideology I had built around myself began to crack.

Then something else happened to me. I do not remember any specific event that caused me to do it, but for some reason I began reading the Bible again. Even though I considered myself a Christian, I had never enjoyed reading the Bible. I had, of course, used some verses out of context to support my racist, anti-Semitic views, but the Bible for the most part seemed ancient and esoteric, hard to understand. I had tried to read it before but got bored and quit after the first few chapters.

This time things were different. Amazingly different.

This time as I read the New Testament, it seemed to be ablaze with light and life, with words that spoke directly to me. The more I read, the more convinced I became that I was lost, separated from God by my sin. I soon realized that the profession of faith in Christ I had made when I was in my teens had not brought me to salvation. I had merely given mental assent to truth about Christ, but had not committed myself to Him or turned from my sins.

As I read the sixteenth chapter of Matthew, one verse in particular burned its way into my soul: "For what shall it profit a man, if he shall gain the whole world, and lose his own soul?" (verse 26 KJV).

As soon as I read those words, I knew that was exactly what I had been doing. I had been trying to gain the world at the expense of my own soul. I saw in the words of that verse my own reflection—the reflection of a wretched and violent man, a man willing to hurt others in defense of an empty and perverted philosophy. I saw the reflection of a man who was arrogant and self-centered, an ungrateful son who returned the love his parents offered him with cold indifference. I saw a man who desperately needed to be forgiven for a life of great sin.

For the very first time, I had to admit to myself that my revolutionary lifestyle had been an important source of ego-gratification. I had been a big man in radical right-wing circles, and even though "the cause" meant a great deal to me, it was just as important that I get recognition and that people respect me and admire me. Had I been willing to hurt others because it would make me look good to my friends on the radical right? The terrible truth was—yes, I had been.

As I saw myself as I really was, I broke down and sobbed. I had always been strong—someone who would not break down in the face of police pressure to talk, who would not hesitate to put his life on the line for the cause. But seeing my own wickedness in light of the love of God broke me completely, and I wept like a baby.

At first the tears I cried were tears of bitterness and sadness because of what I had done with my life. But as I surrendered my heart to Christ and committed my life to Him, they were transformed into tears of joy. In the moment that I gave my life to Christ, a tremendous weight was lifted from my shoulders. I felt wonderful.

I was still locked in a tiny prison cell. But for the first time in my life, I was free.

Living in the Light

John Perkins

Pasadena, California

A lot has changed in this country since the early 1970s, especially in states like Mississippi. Many of the old symbols of prejudice and segregation, thankfully, have disappeared. In public places you will no longer find water fountains or restrooms labeled *Colored*, and that is very good. The U.S. government said that those outward symbols of racism had to be removed, and they were. At first there was quite a bit of objection on the part of white people who did not want to drink out of the same fountain we drank from. But gradually people got used to the changes, and these days nobody thinks anything about it.

One sad thing, though, is that those outward symbols of racism were just that—outward symbols and nothing more. The fact that they have disappeared from the scene does not mean for a moment that people's hearts have changed, that racism no longer exists in the United States. If we say, "Things have improved and now everything's fine," we are fooling ourselves like an ostrich with his head stuck in the sand, like Nero fiddling away while Rome burned. Again, I say it is good and necessary that the obvious outward signs of prejudice have disappeared from the American landscape, but we will be much better off when the inward prejudice

139

disappears from the hearts of people—and I am talking about black as well as white.

Another sad thing is that Sunday is still the most segregated day of the week throughout America, especially Sunday morning when people are in church. It always bothered me that it was not the white evangelical Christian churches who were in the forefront of the battle against racial separation in this country. But it really breaks my heart when I look around and see many evangelical churches that have been the most resistant to change.

I remember a conversation that a friend of mine, a black doctor in the South, had with a white colleague. The two men were attending a medical convention and the white doctor started talking about how good things were between the races these days. White and blacks could stay in the same hotels, he said, and eat in the same restaurants. "Who knows," he added, "maybe not too long from now you will even be able to attend our church."

It seems to me the ultimate irony that the very place where bigotry should never have been tolerated to begin with is the last place to give it the boot.

As for me personally, there have been many changes in my life over the last twenty-plus years.

After my night of terror in Brandon, I had to stand trial in the state of Mississippi. They needed to charge me with something, but then, I had not done anything. On February 16, 1970, I appeared before a justice of the peace in the town of Mendenhall. He found me guilty of contributing to the delinquency of a minor and sentenced me to three months in jail and a $300 fine. I appealed, and in a jury trial was found guilty once again. The sentence was upped to four months in jail and a $400 fine.

The minor was an eleven-year-old girl in our church named Georgia Ann Quinn. The state charged that I did "willfully and unlawfully contribute to the delinquency of a minor under the age of sixteen years, whose name is Georgia Ann Quinn, willfully and unlawfully inducing and persuading said minor to enter and remain in the Simpson County Jail contrary to the instructions of Jimmy Griffiths, jailer of Simpson County." Georgia Ann had been with us in the jail along with her whole family.

The trial itself was a travesty. Attorneys for the state of Mississippi painted me as one of the sleaziest, most despicable characters ever to go on trial in that state. To hear them tell it, I might as well have been out robbing banks and shooting people. John Dillinger had nothing on me. It was terrible to have to sit there and listen to them tear me apart, but I knew I had done nothing wrong, and I knew God was on my side.

After the verdict came down, my lawyers appealed to the Mississippi Supreme Court. Because of certain improprieties in the way my trial was conducted, the Supreme Court referred the matter back to the lower court with two options: Give Perkins a new trial or drop the charges.

The end result of all this legal maneuvering was that a bargain was struck in which I would plead guilty to a lesser charge of disturbing the peace and be ordered to pay a small fine. In a sense I had lost. I had not done anything wrong, but I was still found guilty. On the other hand I had won. I was a black man who had fought the system in Mississippi and come close to being exonerated. I would not spend any more time in jail. That was a good sign for blacks throughout the state. We could stand up for ourselves and seek justice in the courts.

In the years that followed, Voice of Calvary continued to grow and impact hundreds of lives with the good news of Christ's love. We built houses. We started cooperatives. We organized community-wide events for our children. And we told everyone we came in contact with about the abundant life available only through Jesus Christ.

We knew times of tremendous joy and success, and had numerous setbacks and heartbreaks. But through everything that happened, we had the joy and satisfaction of knowing that we were engaged in God's work and following His call.

As the years went by, God began to tell Vera Mae and me that our work in Mississippi was finished.

Notice that I did not say *the* work was done; I said *our* work was done. It was time to relinquish the reins of leadership and move on. This time God was telling us to return to California.

It had been difficult to leave California for Mississippi in the first place, and now we found it just as difficult to do the reverse. For despite the painful experiences, the heartaches suffered there, the bloody battles we had had to fight, we had grown to love Mississippi. Our children had grown up there. We had many wonderful friends there—and no friendship is so strong or lasting as one that has been forged in the fire. We had been through a lot with many of these people. We had stood by them and they had stood by us. It hurt our hearts to have to tell them good-bye.

But there was no mistaking what God was telling us to do, and ultimately the excitement and anticipation of discovering the new thing He had in store for us was stronger than our sorrow at leaving so many loved ones behind. God was calling us to urban southern California to start a work aimed at reaching America's urban areas for Christ, rebuilding the spiritual foundation of America's cities and reclaiming them for His glory.

And so, since 1982, Vera Mae and I have lived in a high-crime area of the city of Pasadena, where I have headed up Harambee Christian Center and the John M. Perkins Foundation for Reconciliation and Development.

The foundation, among its other aims, seeks to build bridges of reconciliation and understanding among various racial and ethnic groups. One of the ways it does this is through our publication, *Urban Family* magazine, which is billed as "the magazine of hope and progress." This magazine reaches into more than twenty thousand homes and is the only national Christian magazine that offers hope to urban families and communities through solution-oriented articles, stories and profiles. It is a call to responsibility, dignity, moral values and reconciliation. In each issue of *Urban Family* are articles like "Ten Ways to Be a Better Father," "How to Get and Keep a Job in the '90s," "Twenty-Five Real Urban Role Models" and "Ten Tips for Single Mothers." It also features people who are living out racial reconciliation—stories like "Can Blacks and Whites Be Neighbors?", "White Boyz in the Hood" and "How to Build an Interracial Friendship."

Our hope is that *Urban Family* will be a stabilizing voice in the midst of the confusion in our inner cities, and give leadership in the quest for racial harmony in this country.

Another way our work at the foundation is beginning to pay dividends is through a unique group of Christians called the Christian Community Development Association (CCDA). For more than twenty years I have traveled around the country trying to inspire and encourage Christians to take up the torch for the poor in their cities and towns. The culmination of those years of work is embodied in CCDA.

In 1989 our foundation called together several of these ministries, organizations and churches to form this unique association. Over the past four years it has grown from 35 to more than 200 grassroots organizational members who live and work among the poor in mostly urban areas.

I believe that for Christians to live and work among the poor is the best answer to the plight of our urban poor. People like those involved in this association are giving leadership to the task of redeeming our cities.

I am delighted that God is allowing us to make a contribution—whether large or small—toward reclaiming America's cities for Him. It ought to be apparent to everybody that America's urban areas are in trouble. They are centers of poverty, crime and drug abuse, including alcoholism.

I can sit in my living room in Pasadena and watch people stagger by who are strung out on drugs or booze. A young man was killed by gang gunfire just across the street from our house. But we are working to be the light of the world in the middle of much darkness. We may be a small beginning, but we are a beginning nonetheless and are determined to do what we can, with God's help.

But then, of course, not everyone wants to see things changed. We paid a price for what we did in Mississippi, and we have paid a price in California, too. Our foes have changed, but their tactics have not.

In Mississippi we received threatening phone calls in the middle of the night and were afraid that a bomb would be put into our car. In California our house has been firebombed twice.

(Thankfully, we were able to put out the fire before the house was destroyed, and there were no serious injuries.) In Mississippi our opponents hated us because of our attempts to bring justice and equality to the state's black residents. In California our opponents are black drug dealers poisoning the minds and bodies of young men and women with their drugs. They hate us because they fear that our presence in the community will cut into their profits.

I hope they are correct—that we *will* cut into their profits. For far too long, America's inner cities have been abandoned to drug dealers, pimps, gangsters and the like, and it is 'way past time that we Christians, both black and white, got serious about liberating our communities in the name of Jesus.

You know, the Bible tells us that the Gospel is authenticated by signs and wonders. In biblical times there was possibly no greater sign or wonder than to see a crippled person healed instantly or a blind man regain his sight. Such miracles were powerful evidence for the truth of the Gospel. In today's society I believe there is no greater evidence than white and black Christians working together, walking together and worshiping together without a single hint of racial division between them, united in an effort to win the lost to Christ and lift up the poor and downhearted in His name. If a non-Christian saw a miracle like that, he would have to admit that there was a great, great power behind the Word of God.

I believe it is an awesome display of God's power that Tom Tarrants and I are such good friends. It is ironic to realize that he and I were both active in the civil rights battles taking place in the American South during the late '60s and early '70s, but on diametrically opposed sides. I remember reading in the newspaper about some of the bombing attacks he carried out and knowing at the time that he would have destroyed me and my ministry if that were possible. I also remember reading about his arrest, trial and subsequent escape from prison.

I am making a gross understatement when I say that Tom Tarrants was not someone I was interested in meeting. I am sure he would have felt the same way about me. In fact, I know he would have hated me, and if the love of God would have let me do it, I am sure I would have hated him right back.

I remember the first time I met Tom. I had been invited to Geneva College in Pennsylvania as a guest lecturer and there he was—a tall, soft-spoken white man. After talking to him for a few minutes, I could not believe this was the same man who had done all those terrible things. It was obvious right away that he had been touched and changed by the love of God. Standing before me was an amazing example of what it means to become a new creature in Christ.

I was scheduled to speak to a group of black students that afternoon, and I invited him to say a few words to them. I was not convinced that they would want to hear what he had to say, considering his past, and I did not know what sort of reception he would get. He didn't either, but was quick to accept my invitation.

I do not remember everything he said that day. I do remember his graciousness, his enthusiasm for the Gospel, his words of apology for the things he had believed and said and done. When he was finished, he received a long and loud ovation.

Later that year he came to California and we spent a few days getting to know each other. The better I got to know him, the more I loved him as a brother, and the more impressed and amazed I was by what God had done in his life. Once we would have been the worst of enemies. Now we are the best of friends, brothers in Christ, working hand-in-hand for the sake of the Gospel. I love Tom Tarrants and know he loves me. As far as I am concerned, there could be no greater demonstration of God's power.

This is the sort of thing that can happen when the love of God gets hold of a person's heart. If we look to God as our source of power and strength, we can heal the racial divisions that exist in this land and thereby win thousands, perhaps even millions, of new souls for Jesus Christ.

In the next few chapters of this book, Tom and I will present some practical ways for you and your church to become actively involved in the vitally important work of healing racial animosity. I am thoroughly convinced that this is one of the most important, yet most often overlooked, missions of individual Christians and of the Christian Church today.

I said it in chapter 1 and will say it again: Unless we act now, the future of the entire nation is at stake.

Tom Tarrants

Washington, D.C.

Much has happened since the day I found Jesus Christ in the state penitentiary at Parchman, Mississippi. I want to take a few moments to tell you where I am today and how I got here.

As I write this, I serve as co-pastor of a Christ-centered church in the city of Washington, a church that happens to be racially mixed. We are involved in several missions programs, but one that I am most involved with is our outreach to the inner city of Washington—our own backyard, so to speak. This involves both evangelistic outreach and ministries of compassion and empowerment that seek to touch and transform our city with the love of Christ.

Because Washington is 66 percent black, this involves us with the black community. A number of our people have been involved in outreach to those who live in one of the worst government housing projects in the city. A husband-and-wife team moved into the area to establish contact, thus opening the door for about twenty others to get involved. We are now teaming up with a black church in the area to minister more effectively.

Our society has a way of closing doors to blacks, Hispanics and other minorities, of relegating them to second-class status. It is gratifying to help them open those doors of opportunity and watch them walk through.

I also serve as co-director of the School for Urban Mission, a training program for people interested in evangelistic, discipleship and compassion ministries in our cities. Serving with me is Fletcher Tink, a former professor at Fuller Seminary and leading urbanologist. Our board of advisors includes Dr. Myron Augsburger, Dr. Sam Hines and the Rev. Tom Skinner. Students study with us for one or two semesters and can earn college or seminary credit for course work. Classes are small and courses challenging. The program focuses on spiritual formation and missions in the urban context, along with practical internships. We have been holding classes since 1990 and have seen a number of our students go into ministry in the Washington area.

It is only God's sovereign grace that has changed me from a hate-filled racist into a follower and servant of Jesus Christ. The catalyst for those changes (as I wrote in the last chapter) was that verse of Scripture burning its way into my soul: "For what shall it profit a man . . . ?"

The sudden impact of that question brought me to my knees, and to Christ. From that time on I was different. I knew without a doubt that something wonderful had happened to me, and that I would never be the same.

When I got up from my knees, it was with the realization that the only thing I wanted out of life was to be the person God wanted me to be. It did not matter what my old "friends" thought of me. I was not worried about "the cause." I was interested only in finding and following God's will for my life, whatever that might be.

I did not immediately become an ex-racist. I still had some of those feelings deep down inside. But in the light of God's overwhelming love, those old attitudes did not seem so important anymore.

I began to read the Bible for hours at a time, and I loved it. Every page seemed to contain something I had never seen before, some new truth that spoke directly to me. When I was not reading the Bible, more than likely I was praying—something else I spent hours at every day. I just could not get enough of God or His Word.

Many of the verses I read spoke to me clearly and forcefully about the racist attitudes I had clung to for so long. I realized there was no way I could read a verse like 1 John 4:20 and still hate someone just because he was black or Jewish: "If someone says, 'I love God,' and hates his brother, he is a liar; for he who does not love his brother whom he has seen, how can he love God whom he has not seen?" (NKJV).

How could I believe that any race is inferior to any other in light of Galatians 3:28: "There is neither Jew nor Greek, there is neither slave nor free, there is neither male nor female; for you are all one in Christ Jesus" (NKJV).

The more I read the Bible, the more my old racist attitudes melted away.

Another factor in the changing of those attitudes was that I got to know, like and even admire some of my fellow prisoners who happened to be black. The fact that they were in prison meant they had made mistakes in their lives, as I had, but they befriended me in spite of my past involvement with the Ku Klux Klan.

Getting to know a man like Dr. Luther McCaskill, the prison doctor who was so bright and compassionate, had already made its mark on me. It was difficult to believe in black inferiority in the presence of a man like that.

Then there was Gary, a young black man who was just about my age. I do not remember why Gary was in prison, but I found him to be open and honest and caring. He knew about my racist past but still accepted me as his friend. We spent quite a bit of time together talking about the "great issues" of our day. Gary was still looking for the answer to life's problems, while I had found the answer in the Person of Jesus Christ. The more I got to know Gary, the more I liked him.

The same was true of Douglass Baker, a black attorney who was serving a short term at Parchman. Doug was articulate, extremely well-read and a gifted classical pianist. He was outspoken regarding his racial and political beliefs, but I still loved talking to him because he was such a thinker. I always found myself challenged and stimulated intellectually when Doug and I had one of our discussions. Much of what he said made good sense.

Doug, like Gary, accepted me as his friend despite what he knew of my past. He was also willing to listen when I talked to him about the Lord, even though he was not a Christian at the time. Shortly after he was released from prison, he did surrender his life to Christ and is serving God faithfully today. I do not see him all that often anymore since we live in different parts of the country, but I still consider him a good friend.

During this time I also developed friendships with two left-leaning white prisoners. Vic Nance, a college student, had been a hippie and drug-dealer prior to his incarceration. In prison he accepted the Lord and later went into full-time prison ministry.

Bill Rusk had been a member of the radical left organization Students for a Democratic Society. He was a soft-spoken, intelligent fellow and someone I liked, even though he and I were far apart ideologically.

I know now that God was showing me the width and depth of His love. There had been a time when I had hated with a passion those who disagreed with my view of the world. But here I was becoming best friends with a black attorney who was militant on the issue of civil rights, an ex-hippie drug abuser and a leftist radical. It was a strange cast of characters, to be sure, but I knew God was bringing us together to teach me something about myself, as well as about others.

It did not take long for word of my conversion to get out. Naturally, some people were skeptical and thought I was using religion to get better treatment for myself. I did not really blame them. But others were willing to wait and see if my faith was real.

Ken Dean, for example, a Baptist minister who headed up the Mississippi Council on Human Relations, came to see me several times. Ken was a political liberal and someone I would have hated before Christ took control of my life. I had always figured that a liberal was a Communist-sympathizer interested only in taking away personal freedoms in the name of big government. But Ken was a good man who genuinely wanted to help people, and I found myself growing to like him in spite of our differences.

Ken brought a man by the name of Al Binder to the prison to meet me. Binder, who was Jewish, had taken a year off from his law practice to devote himself to efforts to break up the Klan in Mississippi. Naturally, because he knew about my history of violence aimed at Jews and blacks, he was among the skeptics when he heard stories about my conversion. But eventually he and I became friends.

Another man who came to see me—once again—was Frank Watts, the FBI agent who had previously expressed an interest in my spiritual well-being. He was sent to the prison by J. Edgar Hoover, who thought I was trying to use religion as a means of finding a way to escape. But Watts was still genuinely interested in my spiritual well-being and was delighted about the changes

that had taken place in my life. As a matter of fact, he and his partner, Jack Rucker, both told me they had never seen such a drastic
change in someone's personality or outlook.

But they wanted to see "fruit worthy of repentance." They knew
I had a great deal of inside information pertaining to groups such
as the White Knights of the Ku Klux Klan, the Minutemen, etc. If
I was truly sorry for what I had done, they said, why didn't I use
what I knew to put some of my former comrades behind bars?
Surely I could see that that was the proper thing to do, especially
when putting those men behind bars would prevent them from
carrying out further acts of violence. They hinted that I might be
given special consideration if I told them everything I knew.

My response was that I had no use at all for someone who would
betray his friends to obtain personal advantage. I could not see
how it would glorify Christ for me to turn against those people,
even though I no longer agreed with what they were doing.
Besides, it seemed to me that the authorities had already pretty
much broken the back of groups like the White Knights. They just
were not that much of a threat anymore.

I felt bad that Frank Watts was disappointed in my reaction to
his request for information, but would not be budged from my
position. I would not "rat" on my friends before I was a Christian
and I would not do it now.

In this I was still more influenced by the attitudes of my old life
than by the Bible, but I was too new in the faith to know it.

Unfortunately, some of my old friends in the Klan were not so
sure I would not talk now, and wanted to make sure there was no
way I could. They wanted me dead. I suspect they took a dim view
of my public repudiation of the Klan as an anti-Christian organization. No doubt some of the top leaders were especially angry
about some letters I had written to them explaining why we had
been wrong in our actions and urging them to surrender their lives
to Christ. I should have known they would not listen to me, of
course, but in the zealous aftermath of my conversion I was hope-
ful that I could get them to see the light.

Instead, they saw red. They saw me as a traitor, and they knew
how to deal with traitors. They dispatched one of their attorneys

to the prison, where he offered one of my fellow inmates $2,500 to help me have a fatal accident.

Fortunately for me, this fellow got drunk one night while he was playing cards with some other inmates and decided that one of them was trying to cheat him. He became furious and started chasing the alleged cheater with a very large, very sharp knife. Somehow I managed to stop him and get him to sit down. When he sobered up, he was so grateful that I had prevented him from committing a murder that he told me all about the Klan plot on my life. He had enough corroborating details that I knew he was telling me the truth, and I was grateful to God for the way He had worked things out to save my life.

About a year after I met Christ, E. R. Moody, the sergeant in charge of the prison's maximum security unit, asked me if I would like to do some clerical work in his office. Naturally I jumped at the chance. For one thing, it meant escaping the tedium of life in a small cage, at least for a few hours every day. For another thing, it gave me a chance to prove that I could be trusted. I found out later that Sergeant Moody had jeopardized his own career to help me. After pleading my case to his superiors, he was told that he could hire me. But if I tried to escape or caused trouble in any way, he would be fired. Moody was taking quite a chance, especially considering that he knew all about my past and my previous escape. But he believed that I had been touched and changed by God's power and was willing to give me a chance, no matter what anyone else said about it.

Very slowly but surely, God was spinning the gears into motion that would ultimately bring about my early release from prison.

Things shifted into second gear in the spring of 1972, when the newly appointed superintendent of the prison, John Collier, made an inspection tour of the maximum security unit. I was working in Sergeant Moody's office when he went through the cellblock, but when he saw the Christian books and other materials in my cell, he wanted to meet me.

He came down to the office, introduced himself and asked if I was a Christian. He was pleased to hear about what the Lord was doing in my life and wished me well. Collier himself was a devout

Christian, outspoken regarding his faith in Christ, and I was impressed by the way he talked to me—like one brother to another, in spite of the very different circumstances that had brought us into the prison.

A few months later, at the request of the prison chaplains and psychologist, I was granted trusty status by John Collier. Two months later I was released from the maximum security unit and allowed to move into a garage apartment in the back of Collier's home on the prison grounds. I was also given a job as a clerk in the chaplain's office.

Were these changes unusual? More than that, they were unheard of. There was no way any of this could be happening. But it was, and I knew Who was causing it.

I loved working in the chaplain's office. Among my other duties, I sometimes accompanied the chaplains when they made their rounds within the prison, and even got to go along on speaking engagements to the outside world. I also taught regular Bible studies for the other prisoners and was thrilled to see some of their lives changed by the power and love of Christ.

More and more I wanted to go back to school—to college and seminary. I wanted to serve Christ in some way. In fact, it was more than something I wanted. It was something God wanted for me.

In the summer of 1974, thanks to the efforts of several friends, including Ken Dean and Bill Hollowell, the new prison superintendent, I took the Scholastic Aptitude Test and applied for admission into several colleges. I was eventually accepted by Duke University in North Carolina, Earlham College in Indiana and Rutgers University in New Jersey. I was excited and ready to go. The prison psychologist had recommended my release. People I had once considered my enemies had expressed their support for what I was trying to do. Even the lieutenant governor had indicated he was all for it.

Everybody was for me, it seemed, except the governor. In a televised news conference, he said he just did not think I was ready.

Naturally I was devastated, and had to work my way through a time of depression and anger. Then the Lord seemed to be telling me to relax, that it was all in His hands and that I would be released from prison in His time. It did not really matter whether the governor thought I was ready for release. What mattered was whether God thought I was ready, and when He did, I would be set free. It was really that simple.

It was not until nearly two years later that the Lord began to open the door. This time, in the spring of 1976, a work-release program was instituted in Mississippi as a means of reducing overcrowding in state prisons, which was terrible. (The prison at Parchman was designed for a maximum of 1,900 prisoners, yet more than 2,600 men were crowded into it.) To ease conditions, a new state law provided for the closely supervised early release of those who were not considered a threat to society.

About this time I met Dr. Leighton Ford, an associate of Billy Graham, when he came to the prison to preach. Through the efforts of Dr. Ford and the chaplains, I was able to be released from prison for two weeks to travel to Washington to attend a seminar sponsored by Charles Colson's Prison Fellowship. It was unheard of for a prisoner to get time off to do something like that, but God opened all the doors for me so I could go. It was another in a series of life-changing experiences.

At one point during the conference, I was in the kitchen of Fellowship House talking with someone when Chuck Colson came in and said he wanted to introduce me to Eldridge Cleaver, the former head of the radical Black Panther Party. I had heard that Cleaver had become a Christian but still had to ask Colson in a joking way, "Are you sure this guy's saved?" Colson assured me that Cleaver had indeed met the Lord, and a few moments later I found myself shaking hands warmly with a man I would have hated passionately—and I am sure he would have hated me just as passionately—only a few years before. The love of God is an amazing thing!

I met four other men during that two-week stay in Washington who were to have a significant influence on my life: Colson himself; Senator Harold Hughes, a liberal Democrat from Iowa; Dr. Richard Halverson; and a black man by the name of John Staggers. All these men have had a powerful effect on me—but especially John Staggers and Dick Halverson. Staggers, who died a few years ago, was one of the most remarkable Christians I have ever known.

John was a big, portly guy who always had a warm, friendly smile. John had served as special assistant to the mayor of Washington, D.C., was an associate professor of sociology at Howard University and had been director of the Model Cities program. He became a Christian relatively late in life, but when he met the Lord, he *really* met the Lord. He was totally committed to Christ and put God's will above all else in life.

When John, who was one of the teachers for the Prison Fellowship seminar, heard that I was going to be in his class, his reaction was pretty much what mine had been when Colson wanted to introduce me to Eldridge Cleaver. Despite his initial reservations about me, however, he never showed me anything but Christian love, and we hit it off immediately.

That was the beginning of what for me was a very fruitful relationship. Years later, when I moved to the Washington, D.C., area, John Staggers was one of the first people I went to see, since I knew I needed his wisdom and guidance. I learned much about black-white relationships from him, and much about my own relationship with Christ. I dearly loved that man, and it was a terrible loss when he died.

Dick Halverson has also been a great blessing in my life. For many years Dick was senior pastor at Fourth Presbyterian Church and chairman of the board of World Vision. For the past decade he has been chaplain of the U.S. Senate. But those really are not the important things about Dick. The remarkable thing is that in spite of these distinctions, he remains a radical disciple of Jesus Christ, a man of great humility whose passion in life is to be like the Christ he preaches.

Anyway, those two weeks at the Prison Fellowship seminar were wonderful, but they went by all too fast and it was time for me to return to prison. As I returned I was hoping that Mississippi's new work-release program would benefit me. But nothing happened right away.

Once again, a number of friends and acquaintances went to bat for me. Dr. Chester Quarles, director of the law enforcement program at the University of Mississippi, sponsored me. It took several months before I came up for consideration, but finally I was notified that I had been scheduled for an interview with the prison warden—an interview that for me could make all the difference in the world. But this time I realized that my future was not in the warden's hands; my future was in God's hands.

When the big day finally came, the warden was tough. He had a hundred questions and fired them at me in machine-gun style. It was more of an interrogation than an interview, and nothing in his demeanor made me think he was pleased by what he was hearing from me. Since he was a self-proclaimed atheist, my Christian faith did not impress him. The tough questions came at me for thirty minutes or more.

Then, abruptly, the interview ended. The warden sat looking at me for a moment, then announced matter-of-factly that he was going to let me go.

"I'm not going to release you because of your religion," he said, "because I don't think it's worth five cents. But I do believe you have changed and deserve a chance to make something of yourself. That's why I'm going to release you."

Little did he know that a number of believers had been praying earnestly for this interview for some time, asking God to release me for the ministry I was called to.

Come the following Monday, December 13, 1976, after spending eight years of my life in this prison, I would be a free man.

God opened the doors to me at the University of Mississippi through the sponsorship of Dr. Chester Quarles. My years there were good. I made many friends, both black and white, and enjoyed my studies. The believers there were a great help and blessing to me as I continued to grow spiritually.

In 1978 I moved to Washington, D.C., at the encouragement of Doug Coe. Doug was a strong influence for Christ in my life. Like his close friend Dick Halverson, Doug had a passion for Jesus Christ. The original plan was for me to work under Doug in a ministry of teaching and discipling, and to finish my degree at George Washington University or American University. As it turned out,

I got into campus ministry, married and went on to seminary, graduating in 1986. During those years I met two other black leaders who were destined to have a powerful impact on my life for Christ: Dr. Sam Hines and Dr. Tom Skinner. Both men are apostles of reconciliation. And both men befriended me warmly and have been good friends and wise teachers over the years, helping me grasp the truths of the faith in new, life-changing ways.

It has been a strange but wonderful pilgrimage over the years. It seems that God has met me at every turn with His grace, giving me favor and blessing I did not deserve. I do not profess to understand it; I just thank God for it. His grace is beyond all comprehension and leaves us in wonder and astonishment.

Part

Developing a Strategy for Reconciliation

The Model for Reconciliation

Tom Tarrants

As we now shift our mental gears to focus on strategies for racial reconciliation, I have a keen sense of still being very much a learner. While I have black friends from whom I have learned much over the years, I have neither the richness of experience nor the depth of understanding that come from years of working together day to day in a one-on-one long-term committed relationship. (This is modeled powerfully in such books as *More than Equals* by Spencer Perkins and Chris Rice, and *Breaking Down Walls* by Raleigh Washington and Glen Kehrein.)

What I bring to the table is a combination of experiences, insights and observations gained from good friendships with several black brothers, especially John Staggers, Dr. Sam Hines, Dr. Tom Skinner and Dr. John Perkins. Much of what I have learned has been caught as much as taught. I also offer the fruit of some years of biblical and theological reflection on the issue.

Defining the Problem

If we are serious about developing strategies for racial reconciliation, we must first take the time and effort to define the problem clearly. This may seem obvious, but I suspect that many of us,

159

especially whites, do not take enough time to do this. As a result, we are often dealing with symptoms instead of root causes. Symptoms need to be treated, of course; but to find a lasting solution, we must address root causes. If we are always dealing with symptoms, we will see little substantial progress, become discouraged and give up.

Looking for the Root Cause

This is very much a case of bad news and good news. All the problems we face in the world and in our personal lives can be traced back, in the broadest sense, to one cause: the alienation of men and women from God. We see this in the opening chapters of Genesis in which Adam and Eve, through pride and unbelief, chose to disobey God and assert their will against His. Our alienation from God begins here and precipitates alienation from our fellow human beings, seen in Cain's angry murder of his brother, Abel.

Since that time, man has come into the world alienated from God and therefore from his fellow man. Racial and ethnic strife are simply manifestations of this great human tragedy. Whether it is black versus white, Jew versus Arab, Japanese versus Korean, the root cause is alienation from God.

This is the bad news. And unfortunately it gets worse.

If the root cause of ethnic strife is alienation from God (and the Bible affirms that it is), then there can be no real, lasting solution to the problem in this present world. The only place in the Bible where we see a solution is in the book of Revelation, where we are given a glimpse of what life in the world to come will be like. One of its glorious features is universal love and harmony among all God's people—black, white, brown, yellow and red—as in Revelation 7:9–10:

> After this I looked and there before me was a great multitude that no one could count, from every nation, tribe, people and language, standing before the throne and in front of the Lamb. They were wearing white robes and were holding palm branches in their

hands. And they cried out in a loud voice: "Salvation belongs to our God, who sits on the throne, and to the Lamb."

Not until we are in the world to come will we experience life without racism. But that does not mean that nothing can be done on this side of eternity. Jesus warned us to expect stumbling blocks (Matthew 18:7) but did not see them as an excuse for capitulation. Unfortunately some of us blacks and whites have concluded just that and feel there is nothing we can do.

But to draw such a conclusion is both premature and unbiblical.

Looking for the Solution

Here is where the good news comes in. Although there is no universal solution to racial alienation this side of eternity, God intends that there be authentic and visible examples of His coming Kingdom in this present world *through the Church*. This unquestionably includes racial reconciliation.

Paul teaches us this principle using the case of Jews and Gentiles. In Ephesians we read:

> Therefore, remember that formerly you who are Gentiles by birth and called "uncircumcised" by those who call themselves "the circumcision" (that done in the body by the hands of men)—remember that at that time you were separate from Christ, excluded from citizenship in Israel and foreigners to the covenants of the promise, without hope and without God in the world. But now in Christ Jesus you who once were far away have been brought near through the blood of Christ. *For he himself is our peace, who has made the two one and has destroyed the barrier, the dividing wall of hostility,* by abolishing in his flesh the law with its commandments and regulations. *His purpose was to create in himself one new man out of the two, thus making peace, and in this one body to **reconcile** both of them to God through the cross, by which he put to death their hostility* (Ephesians 2:11–16, emphasis added).

This reconciliation of Jew and Gentile was every bit as radical and seemingly impossible as that of blacks and whites today. The

Jews hated Gentiles, held them in contempt and called them "dogs," the equivalent of *nigger* today.

A careful study of this entire chapter of Ephesians, especially the verses immediately preceding this passage, makes clear that salvation by grace through faith in Jesus Christ is intended to be manifested visibly in reconciled communities (local churches) composed of both Jew and Gentile, black and white, red and yellow. Jesus Himself is our basis for this unity and peace, not our race, ethnicity, social status, cultural distinctives or religious background.

But before we go further, let's pause to examine the meaning of the word *reconcile*. Although reconciliation has seldom been a sermon topic in evangelical churches, it is a word being used more and more in evangelical circles today. I first heard it when I was a young believer and knew little about the Bible. In those days it was used widely by people on the theological left who saw the need for people to be reconciled to one another but saw little need for them to be reconciled to God. I identified *reconcile*, then, as a liberal word. And because I saw personal salvation as fundamental to all else in life, I paid little attention to the word, even though I read it many times in 2 Corinthians.

This was unfortunate because, as Dr. Sam Hines later helped me to see, reconciliation is one of the most basic and significant ideas in all the Bible. Far from being a liberal word, it lies at the very heart of evangelical theology. As Dr. J. I. Packer wrote in *God's Words*, "Of all the great words that the New Testament uses to explain the saving work of Christ—redemption, justification, and the rest—reconciliation is perhaps the most full and expressive."

What, then, does the Bible mean by the word *reconcile?* The basic meaning of the Greek root from which we get this word means "to change or exchange." Long before New Testament times, it was used in classical Greek to describe the change of relations that occurred in the bringing together of estranged parties.

In the New Testament the word is used exclusively by Paul, and means first and foremost God's act of resolving the estrangement between Himself and humanity through the death of Christ. This is the clear meaning in key passages where it is used, such as

Romans 5:10: "For if, when we were God's enemies, we were *reconciled* to him through the death of his Son, how much more, having been *reconciled*, shall we be saved through his life!" And 2 Corinthians 5:18–19 (emphasis added): "All this is from God, who *reconciled* us to himself through Christ and gave us the ministry of reconciliation: that God was *reconciling* the world to himself in Christ, not counting men's sins against them. And he has committed to us the message of *reconciliation*."

Because of His great love for us, God took the initiative and made the first step in reconciling us to Himself. We are sometimes inclined to meet our enemies halfway to be reconciled, but not so with God. He went all the way; He gave one hundred percent. When we were alienated from Him through sin and unable to restore the relationship, He took the initiative to reconcile us to Himself by sending Jesus to bear the penalty of our sins on the cross. This is the heart and soul of reconciliation: It is God's idea, not man's, and is at the very center of God's plan for man and the creation.

First and foremost, then, reconciliation is concerned with personal salvation in Jesus Christ. We must always remember this, lest we begin to use the word simply to describe human relationships or as a slogan for social activism.

But reconciliation with God does not end with personal salvation, as we evangelicals have tended to make it. Quite the contrary! As our passage in Ephesians makes clear, God intends the fruit of reconciliation with Him to be reconciliation with our fellow man—reconciliation with all those from whom we are alienated, especially our enemies. This mighty salvation breaks through all kinds of boundaries. As Paul says in Galatians 3:26–28: "You are all sons of God through faith in Christ Jesus, for all of you who were baptized into Christ have clothed yourselves with Christ. There is neither Jew nor Greek, slave nor free, male nor female, for you are all one in Christ Jesus."

Reconciliation with our fellow man, then, is not some nice fringe benefit that may or may not accompany salvation, as many of us whites are inclined to think. Rather, it is a fundamental part of God's plan and design. God's purpose is expressed by Paul in

Ephesians 3:10: "His intent was that now, through the church, the manifold wisdom of God should be made known to the rulers and authorities in the heavenly realms." The power of Christ's work on the cross to break down the barriers that divide humanity is one way God's wisdom is displayed.

It is also God's plan that all who are reconciled to Him become living examples of that reconciliation as ambassadors of Christ, calling people to be reconciled with God and one another (see 2 Corinthians 5:18–20). In this display of God's grace and supernatural power in the Church, Jesus is glorified, people are saved and God's Kingdom revealed. Reconciliation between believers, racial or otherwise, is made possible by and is the fruit of that prior reconciliation with God. This means that the issue of racial reconciliation is an issue to be resolved visibly in the local church. We must lead the way for the world.

It is not uncommon for us white evangelicals to see racial reconciliation (when we think about it at all) as something peripheral to the Gospel. Scripture gives it a much higher priority. Faithful Gospel ministry will result in conversions among people across all boundaries of race, class and culture. Like a sweeping prairie fire, the Gospel will jump all the firebreaks and ignite everything in its path. This supernatural action is an authenticating mark of the truth and is God's way of demonstrating here and now the nature of His coming Kingdom.

Surely Jesus had this in mind when He commissioned His disciples (which includes us) to "make disciples of all nations" (Matthew 28:19). The Greek word used for *nations* here is *ethne*, which means "nations, peoples." The root *ethnos* is the source of our word *ethnic*.

No one can seriously question that Jesus intends for us to take the Gospel to persons of all ethnic, racial and national groups.

A good way to confirm this point is to look at the lives of those closest to Jesus who best understood what He meant. Luke tells us that the first outpouring of the Spirit at Jerusalem touched Jews "from every nation under heaven" (Acts 2:5). This lit a torch whose flame was to sweep the Roman Empire. For several years, however, the Christian faith remained a movement within Judaism, and apparently proponents saw nothing wrong with that. Their prejudices were so strong and their vision so limited that it never occurred to them that Jesus' outreach among the Samaritans (see John 4) might portend things to come. But it did. So comfortable had they become that God had to allow persecution to scatter the Jerusalem church. And part of that scattering took Philip to Samaria, of all places, where he began to preach.

Philip's preaching was so empowered by the Holy Spirit and authenticated by miraculous signs that many believed. This took the Gospel beyond narrow Jewish provincialism into the camp of their much-despised, half-breed brothers. Still the leadership did not get the message. Finally the Holy Spirit gave Peter an extraordinary vision and sent him to the Roman centurion Cornelius, a full-blooded Gentile. As Peter preached, the Spirit fell upon the group, bringing them all to salvation in Christ and even giving them the same gift of tongues that Peter had experienced at Pentecost. At last Peter understood, and later helped the other leaders in Jerusalem to understand as well: The Gospel is for *all* nations, just as Jesus had said.

Meanwhile, God was also on the move elsewhere. Believers had been scattered because of the persecution that followed Stephen's martyrdom. Some went to Antioch, a city that Josephus tells us had a mixed population. Here the followers of Jesus were led to preach to the Gentiles, with many conversions resulting. The die was now cast; there would be questions to resolve but no turning back.

Next, Paul would take the Gospel throughout the Gentile world, planting churches everywhere he went. There can be no doubt that as the Gospel penetrated the cosmopolitan centers of the Empire, including Rome itself, the majority of converts came from among the lower class of society, which was composed of people from a variety of ethnic backgrounds.

The Church of the first four centuries has much to teach us about what it means to know, love and follow Jesus Christ as Lord. People of all backgrounds became, through faith in Christ, part of the Kingdom of God. And they demonstrated this in their life together in the Church, where their love for one another was legendary, even among the pagans. Their love also reached out to the poor, the oppressed, the suffering and the downtrodden, and multitudes came to Christ because of it.

The Problem with the Solution

But that was then and this is now. We live in a society in which things are very different. Not simply different kinds of people, or different problems, or different needs, but a different Church. As Dick Halverson once observed, Christianity began as a relationship with Jesus Christ. The Greeks made it into a philosophy, the Romans made it into a religion, the Europeans made it into a civilization, and now the Americans have made it into an enterprise.

The fundamental problem in racial reconciliation, as well as in a good many other issues we face, is the Church herself. I do not say this as one who has taken the easy road of writing off the Church, but as one who believes in and is committed to the Church. I am committed to the Church because Jesus is committed to it. In spite of Satan's unremitting opposition and man's weakness, despite many problems in the Church now and in the past, Jesus is building His Church, and He will ultimately prevail! In pitched battles through the centuries, the forces of Satan have at times seemed to have gained the upper hand. But then God moves forward, often in the darkest hour, using unknown people in unexpected ways.

We are at such a dark hour today in relation to racial reconciliation and a number of other issues.

What is the problem that compromises the Church? After many years of exposure to churches of almost every denomination and stream in the Body of Christ, in the United States and abroad, I have concluded that most problems in the Church, including racism, arise from one of two root causes: lack of true conversion or lack of total commitment to Jesus Christ. Take any problem you wish and trace it back to its root. It will most likely be one or the other of these causes.

These are not new problems. For the first three hundred years of the Church, the social ostracism and intermittent persecution from authorities ensured that few would profess faith in Christ and identify with Him unless they were genuinely converted and committed. There were exceptions, of course, even in New Testament times, but these do not appear to have been numerous.

But after 313 A.D. things changed when the emperor Constantine I ended state persecution and adopted the Christian faith. (Evidence for the genuineness of his conversion is confusing.) As a result, Christianity became fashionable and the Church began to be flooded with opportunists. This is often described as the fall of the Church. Many unbelievers identified themselves as believers for personal aggrandizement. This continued for centuries, giving impetus to various reform movements within the Catholic Church. Eventually the Reformation came, doing much good but not really solving the problems. They continue with us today.

Let's look at each of these problems in turn—lack of true conversion and lack of total commitment to Jesus Christ—and explore how they relate to the problem of racial reconciliation.

First, **true conversion.**

Sadly, there is much vagueness and confusion today about what it means to be genuinely converted to Jesus Christ. Most of the cause for this rests squarely on the shoulders of those leaders (pastors, theologians, laymen) who, for a variety of reasons, subscribe to and propagate what amounts to a less-than-biblical view of salvation. In some cases they are bound by ritualism or formalism or traditionalism; in others, doctrinal error. Still others, driven by ambition for "success" in ministry (read: numerical growth), have adopted a pragmatism that softens the Gospel message to make it more palatable. Whatever the cause, the result is the same: many unconverted church members who think they are saved.

Such people, lacking the Holy Spirit's power for godly thinking and living, lead lives little different from their unsaved neighbors. This blurring of the distinction between those who know God and those who do not has compromised the identity and witness of the Church to the watching world. What does this have to do with racial reconciliation? Simple. If you do not love God, you cannot really love your neighbor.

Both John Perkins and his son Spencer tell how hard it was for them to believe that white people could be Christians because of their hatred of blacks. You can be sure there are plenty of other blacks and whites who have the same reaction to so-called Christians, not only on race but on a host of other issues, and reject Christ because of it.

Evidence of this confusion about genuine salvation can be seen in research from the Gallup organization and the Barna Group, where the attitudes and behaviors of a large percentage of those calling themselves Christians are no different from those professing no faith at all.

A number of years ago as a student at the University of Mississippi, long before I knew of Gallup or Barna, I set out to explore this hypothesis. (In traveling around the state of Mississippi with the prison chaplain, I had shared my testimony and preached in a number of churches of different denominations, and begun to wonder how many people in the average church were genuinely converted.) As a major project in a sociology course, I researched and designed a 100-plus-item questionnaire to distinguish between probable born-again believers and probable non-born-again believers among those who called themselves Christians. The instrument measured religious beliefs, experiences and practices, along with intrinsic vs. extrinsic motivation, and was administered to about 150 college students.

Among a number of interesting findings was the fact that while ninety percent claimed to be Christians, fewer than ten percent said they would go to heaven because of what Jesus did on the cross. The remainder believed that God would let them into heaven for one of the following three reasons: (1) A loving God would not send anyone to hell; (2) Their good works outnumbered their bad works; or (3) They were sincere in their beliefs.

When such a large representative percentage of professing Christians in the Bible belt do not know even the most basic facts of the Gospel, can we seriously believe that they are saved and able to live godly lives? This is a national tragedy of the grandest proportions—not simply because so many are deceived, but because they misrepresent to others the nature of true Christianity and bring reproach on the name of Jesus Christ. Even worse, few churches are willing to address the issue, lest attendance and giving decline.

What is defective in our understanding of conversion today? A major issue is the way in which Jesus is seen and presented. Jesus is put forth variously as someone to help us solve our problems; to make life better; to bring fulfillment, inner integration and psychological healing; or as the source of health and prosperity. What these emphases have in common is their focus on Jesus as someone to meet *my* personal needs, to provide *me* with physical and emotional benefits. We hear less and less about a Jesus who was God with us and who came to deliver His people from their sins. *Sin* is an old-fashioned, unpopular word these days, and few people want to hear about or deal with it. Since many churches are now market-driven and extremely sensitive to the likes and dislikes of their customers, sin receives little attention.

It is interesting that as the Church has become less and less willing to address sin, she has become more and more open to our therapeutic culture. As John Perkins puts it, we are now hiring psychologists to help us manage our sin and its consequences.

We can thank God, of course, that this is not a universal trend. There are still many churches that preach salvation by grace through faith and present Jesus as the Savior who makes real changes in a person's attitudes, beliefs, values and behavior.

Unfortunately, there are problems even in some of these churches. In some, we are told that the kind of faith needed to receive salvation is only an intellectual assent to the truth about Jesus. Repentance is seen as unnecessary, and to include it with faith is regarded as mixing works with grace.

This is remarkable in light of the clear teaching of Jesus (Mark 1:15), Peter (Acts 2:38) and Paul (Acts 20:21) that both faith and repentance are necessary for salvation. It is also strange in light of John's Gospel, where the Greek word for *faith, pistis/pisteuo,* does not mean mere intellectual assent but also carries the idea of commitment and change. In John's Gospel the concept of repentance is clearly present, even if the word itself is not. For John, faith means repentant faith. Dr. J. I. Packer's comment in his book *Concise Theology* on this sort of thinking sums up the matter well: "The idea that there can be saving faith without repentance, and that one can be justified by embracing Christ as Savior while refusing Him as Lord, is a destructive delusion."

This easy believism is certainly not new. It has been around since the days of the apostle Paul. More recently it was a major problem in pre-Hitler German Lutheranism. In those days it evoked a powerful response from the theologian Dietrich Bonhoeffer, who coined the phrase *cheap grace* to describe it. Cheap grace, said Bonhoeffer in *The Cost of Discipleship*,

> means grace as a doctrine, a principle, a system. It means the forgiveness of sins proclaimed as a general truth, the love of God taught as the Christian conception of God. An intellectual assent to that idea is held to be of itself sufficient for the remission of sins. . . . In such a church the world finds a cheap covering for its sins; no contrition is required, still less any real desire to be delivered from sin.

Cheap grace is

> the grace which amounts to the justification of sin without the justification of the repentant sinner who departs from sin and from whom sin departs.

Cheap grace is

> the grace we bestow on ourselves. . . . Cheap grace is the preaching of forgiveness without requiring repentance, baptism without church discipline, communion without confession. Cheap grace is grace without discipleship, grace without the cross, grace without Jesus Christ, living and incarnate.

This is certainly a problem in America today. And it means that we need to be clear as to what the Bible teaches about the nature and effect of the Gospel, and the need for both faith and repentance in salvation.

What do we mean by faith and repentance? Far from being simple optimism or even intellectual assent, saving faith involves *believing* that Jesus of Nazareth is the Son of God, that

He died for our sins and was raised from the dead, and it means *trusting* Him as one's Savior. Repentance, on the other hand, is not mere sorrow, regret or remorse, as is often thought, but an awakening to the sinfulness of our sin, along with a resolution to turn from it.

It may help to think of faith and repentance as opposite sides of the same coin. One could say that faith is *turning to Christ from sin*, while repentance is *turning from sin to Christ*. Both repentance and faith are always present in true conversion and so inextricably bound up with one another that they cannot be separated.

Why do I make such a big issue about this? For one thing, I speak from the experience of having been an example of cheap grace, or easy believism. For years I identified myself as and believed myself to be a Christian—all the while spewing forth the most vitriolic hatred of blacks and Jews. In addition, I lived a life of sinful, fleshly indulgence. My life was a contradiction of all that Christ taught, and it brought great reproach on His name among the unsaved. Simply put, it turned people away from Christ and the Gospel. No doubt some, especially Jews, have taken my "Christianity" as a reason to despise and ignore the claims of Christ.

The same thing happens to a greater or lesser extent whenever unconverted people are called Christians. Even if they are nice people and good citizens, their lives do not demonstrate the love of Jesus. Because of this, the Church of Jesus Christ is increasingly seen as irrelevant to modern life—irrelevant because there is no discernible difference between many of those who claim to be Christians and those who do not.

This should not be surprising, inasmuch as Jesus clearly warns that many (not few) will come to Him at the Judgment expecting to enter heaven only to discover that they were never truly converted (Matthew 7:13–23; 25:31–46).

What has all this to do with racial reconciliation? Simply this: If we are puzzled about why so few professing Christians in America are concerned for racial reconciliation or the poor, part of the answer may be that many are not really Christians at all. One of the greatest challenges we face today is helping the "Christians" come to saving faith.

But lack of true conversion is not the only problem in the Church today. Among many who are true converts of Jesus Christ, there is another problem: **lack of total commitment to Him.**

Jesus commissioned His disciples to go and make new disciples from among every ethnic group, teaching them to *obey* everything He had taught them. Believers are called, in other words, to be fully committed disciples. Jesus never offered an optional plan (as some do today) for those who seek a lower standard or a lesser commitment. He made it quite clear that anyone who meant to be His disciple would have to deny himself or herself, take up the cross and follow Him.

The apostle Paul was following Jesus' standard when he urged the Roman believers, in light of God's grace to them, to present their bodies as a living sacrifice to God (Romans 12:1). This, Paul added, was their reasonable service of worship. Far from being some legalist requirement, such commitment is the fruit of grace cultured in a heart that is grateful for all that God has done for us in Christ.

This comes as bad news to the me-centered ethos of our day. Many of us want to have the comforting hope of salvation after death but live for ourselves until then, getting all the "best" this world has to offer.

As we survey the church scene today, we see two powerful realities. First, that relatively few believers in American churches are living as fully committed disciples of Jesus. And second, that those who *are* living as fully committed disciples of Jesus are making a significant impact on the world. Whether we look to Church history or to the present day, the story is the same: Those making a significant impact on the world for Jesus Christ are those who have radically abandoned themselves to Jesus Christ and seek to live daily under His Lordship, no matter what the cost.

What does this have to do with racial reconciliation? Everything. Addressing this issue carries a significant personal cost and offers little worldly return. It is neither glamorous nor sensational nor "exciting." It seems like a waste of time and energy to many whose goals are elsewhere. It often brings misunderstanding, rejection, persecution. Only as we are fully committed to the Lordship of Jesus Christ are we willing and able to engage in such a difficult, demanding pursuit.

In the broadest sense, then, racial alienation in the Church goes back to these two root problems—lack of true conversion and lack of total commitment. The "remedy" to this state of affairs, to the extent that we can speak of a remedy, is a spiritual awakening or revival in many of our American churches. Not some new seminar or conference, not some humanly engineered program or movement, but an outbreak of repentance that deals with our worldliness, self-indulgence and racial sins. If only we could get the "Christians" saved and the saved committed, it would change the world! Nothing short of such a reviving work of God's Spirit will change the American Church, and this should be our priority in prayer.

Where does this leave us? I once put this question to the late Dr. J. Edwin Orr of Fuller Seminary, a world authority on revival. His wise response was that while human beings cannot bring about a great revival, we can see revival in our own lives and in local churches to the extent that we are willing to repent and obey the light the Holy Spirit has given us.

This is the need of the hour for those who desire to see racial reconciliation. Pray earnestly for revival in the American Church and for repentance in your church and in yourself. Then become active as a peacemaker and reconciler.

12 But What Can I Do About It?

John Perkins

There is nothing America can do to change her past. Enslavement of blacks was a fact of life in this country for hundreds of years, and no magic wand will erase that fact or change all the pain and suffering that went along with it. If there were, I would wave it and make all those slave ships disappear so that none of my ancestors could have been brought to this country that way—sick and suffering and wrapped in chains in the nasty holds of those terrible ships.

Slavery has always been a terrible thing, but the way it was practiced in this country was an all-time low. In ancient Greece and Rome slaves were well-educated and trained to manage a business or run a household. In the United States they were used and treated like animals. They were purposefully kept ignorant. They were forced to do back-breaking labor until they were ready to drop, then beaten mercilessly when they did. Families were torn apart, husbands and wives separated without the slightest thought as to their feelings, and children taken from their parents—babies wrenched from their mothers' arms and never allowed to see either of their parents again. It is hard to imagine that kind of heartache.

Yes, there were some decent men among the slave-owners, some who thought highly of their slaves and treated them well. But that did not change the fact that slavery was an evil institution that remains a blight on the history of our country.

As I said, if I could do something magical to make it so that slavery never existed, I would. But I cannot. Neither can I change the biblical truth that people and countries always reap what they sow. The United States sowed a dangerous crop with slavery, and we are continuing today to reap the consequences.

If I could, I would also undo what happened to me. It is terrible to realize even today that I was harassed, beaten brutally and tortured for no other reason than that the color of my skin happens to be black, and because I was doing my best to spread the message that all people are equal before God and ought to be treated as such.

But just as there is no way to change this country's history, there is no way to change my own history. What happened to me happened, and I cannot change it, any more than I can go back into the past and change the forces and attitudes that caused it to happen.

There is one thing I can do, though, and that is work to change attitudes and situations in America today—to try to bring people of all races and cultures together through the love of Christ, to try to see that the sins of the past are not repeated.

You may remember what Edmund Burke said—that the only thing that evil needs in order to triumph is for good men to do nothing. All of us should feel compelled to do what we can, as Americans and as Christians, to help bring healing between the races.

In their book *Breaking Down Walls*, Raleigh Washington and Glen Kehrein list three important reasons every Christian needs to be involved in building bridges between the races:

1. Because Christ made it a priority.

The historical division between Jews and Gentiles was dissolved by the blood of Christ. Paul refers to this in Ephesians 2:14–15 when he says that Christ is "our peace, who has made both one . . . so as to create in Himself one new man from the two, thus making peace."

2. Because the apostle Paul made it a priority.

In Colossians 3:11 Paul wrote that in Christ there is no difference between Jew and Greek, male and female, circumcised and uncircumcised, because all are now one in Christ. (It is interesting to note that Paul apparently expected people of all races and ethnic backgrounds to worship together side by side. Somewhere in the last 2,000 years of progress, we lost the truth of that vision, especially in the American South.)

3. Because the theological foundation of our faith is reconciliation.

This is so important! The reason Christ was born into a human body in the first place was to bring about our reconciliation to God. We were sinners, lost, separated from God, but Christ made it possible for us to be reconciled to Him. Then He turned right around and appointed us to be His ambassadors, giving us the ability and duty to be reconcilers. He expects us to tell people how they can be reconciled to God through the cross, and He also expects us to reconcile people to people across whatever barriers might divide us—including barriers of race, ethnicity and class.

It is amazing that the apostle Paul could have written those verses from the third chapter of Colossians. There is evidence, after all, that he was something of a racist before the resurrected Jesus met him on the road to Damascus. He was extremely proud of his Jewish heritage and wanted nothing at all to do with Gentiles until God showed him how wrong he was.

The apostle Peter was also something of a racist until God sent him to preach the Gospel to a Gentile named Cornelius. Then Peter said, "I now realize how true it is that God does not show favoritism but accepts men from every nation who fear him and do what is right" (Acts 10:34–35, NIV). Once again I have to say, isn't it sad that it has taken some of us nearly 2,000 years to get the message?

I am pleased that the U.S. sends out more missionaries than any other country. We feel mandated to share the Gospel with the rest of the world, and that is wonderful. The problem is, we do not always understand the Gospel. We sometimes feel that it is a message only to be proclaimed and accepted, and nothing more.

But the Gospel is more than a message to be accepted or rejected. It is a way of life. For us to proclaim the Gospel to others means, first, that we share the good news that we have all been loved, and then that we illustrate that love by the way we live. Thus do we demonstrate Christ's love through what we do as well as what we say. James, the brother of Jesus, put it this way: "If a brother or sister is naked and destitute of daily food, and one of you says to them, 'Depart in peace, be warmed and filled,' but you do not give them the things which are needed for the body, what does it profit?" (James 2:15–16).

That call to reach out a loving hand of assistance to the poorer brother or sister crosses cultural, racial and international barriers. If the Gospel we preach is genuine, it is the power to reconcile alienated men and women to a holy God and to one another across all these barriers. It is the only means and hope for international brotherhood and peace, and the only means and hope for brotherhood and peace between different races and ethnic groups here at home. Some people see reconciliation as a tack-on, but that is wrong. Reconciliation is the heart of the Gospel.

These are three important reasons for doing whatever we can to help bring about racial reconciliation, but to them I would add two more:

4. Because racial harmony will produce spiritual revival.

I am convinced that racial reconciliation is a key to revival because it validates the Gospel. When the time comes that the world can look at the Church and see Christians of all nationalities and skin colors working together, worshiping together and loving one another, a revival of unbelievable proportions will explode all across this land—and from here, all across this planet. It will happen because when people see the love flowing between us, they will know God is alive and well.

I look around today and see successful, powerful churches—churches with ten thousand members and even more. But I see churches whose members for the most part could have been stamped out with a cookie cutter. These are "homogeneous" churches—a church growth expert's dream come true. Most of them are in the more affluent suburbs, and most of them are 99.9 percent white. The members come from the same socioeconomic class and share a common heritage. Some of these churches are growing so fast they are bursting at the seams. They are winning white people and becoming strong, powerful and rich. But they are not carrying out the reconciling work of the Gospel.

Someone is sure to say to me, "Well, John, what do you want me to do—go back to my suburban church and tear it up?"

Of course not. What I want you to do, if you are involved in a church like that, is to stay right there, love those people and help them create a mission strategy, just as you might create a mission strategy to take the Gospel overseas. Only this time your strategy is for the purpose of taking the Gospel—the entire Gospel—into the inner city. I will talk more about this in chapter 14.

5. Because the future of our country depends on racial and ethnic harmony.

Jesus said it: "A house divided against itself cannot stand." As American citizens—never mind as Christians—we owe it to our country to help guide her into a peaceful and prosperous future. Unless we can find a way to bring about racial reconciliation and harmony, that kind of future is an impossibility.

Many people these days have rediscovered their African roots, and I think that is terrific. I am as proud as I can be of my African heritage. But I am not an African; I am an American. Any black American who puts his allegiance to Africa above his allegiance to the U.S. is only hurting himself. Someone says to me, "How can you talk that way? Look at all the ways this country has mistreated our people." And while that is true, the answer is not to turn our backs on her, but to work to make her better.

Many of us, after all, have sacrificed tremendously to build this country. Thousands of us have died in her defense. We have given blood, sweat and pain to build her cities and towns, her highways and her railroads. We have made great contributions in the fields of science, medicine and technology. Most of us have lived here for generations. We have seen our children born here and we have buried our parents here. We have a *right* to say that the U.S.A. is our country, and we have a *responsibility* to help guide and shape her into something better than what she is today.

Believe me when I tell you that I understand why so many blacks have ambivalent feelings about the United States. It is their homeland and they love it, but in many ways America has never treated them right.

I remember, back in my early days in Mississippi, how upset I used to get when I listened to white preachers on the radio. Some of the best-known preachers of the day would rant about what the Communists were up to, and how we had to stand up to them before they swarmed into the United States from Mexico or Cuba. Sometimes I would think, "Why in the world should I be afraid of the Communists?"

After all, no Communist had ever called me a nigger. No Communist had ever refused to allow my son or daughter to attend his school. No group of Communists had ever ganged up on me and beat me half to death simply because my skin was black. No Communist had ever refused to hire me or give me some other economic opportunity because he did not like my color. All those things had been done to me right here in America, and it did not seem likely that life under the Communists could be much worse.

You know, it made me mad that those preachers who were so vivid when it came to painting pictures of the terrible things the Communists were going to do if they came here did not seem to notice what terrible things were already being done in this country to an entire race of people.

Still, despite a history of injustice and racism, despite all the problems that exist here, this is my country. I love her. And I want to help make her what she should and can be for *all* of her people.

But there are questions: What can I do? Where can I start? Can I really make a difference?

The answers to those questions, respectively, are: Plenty; right where you are; and yes, you can.

Specifically, there are six things you must do if you want to be an instrument of racial reconciliation. Here they are:

1. **Acknowledge the existence of the problem and the way it affects you.**
2. **Confess your own guilt.**
3. **Seek God's guidance.**
4. **Be willing to take risks.**
5. **Discover opportunities for action.**
6. **Move beyond saying hello.**

Let's look at the first step: **Acknowledge the existence of the problem and the way it affects you.**

One of the biggest reasons we have not dealt effectively with alienation between the races in this country is that most of us just do not see it. It so surrounds us, and we have put up with it for so long, that it seems normal, and we just do not see how it affects us.

The first of the Twelve Steps of Alcoholics Anonymous is to acknowledge the existence of the problem (in that case, that the person is an alcoholic). It is the same here, in that we cannot overcome the racial divisions in this country without acknowledging that they exist, and that we have all been tainted by racism.

Remember the words of Isaiah: "Woe is me, for I am undone! Because I am a man of unclean lips, and I dwell in the midst of a people of unclean lips" (Isaiah 6:5). Our paraphrase might be: "Woe is me, for I am undone! Because I am a person with racist attitudes, and I dwell in the midst of a people of racist attitudes."

We declare to the world that we are "one nation, under God," but we have never really practiced that. Consider the Southern Baptist Convention, the largest Protestant denomination in the U.S. This church was born out of opposition to emancipation, yet as far as I know has never confessed or apologized for the pro-slavery stance it took. Now our nation has as her two top leaders Bill Clinton and Al Gore, both of whom are members of the Southern Baptist Church, and neither of whom has any understanding in terms of moral conviction about what it means to be a Southern Baptist.

Am I saying that the Southern Baptist Convention should change its name? No. But I do believe that the denomination should at the very least issue a statement of acknowledgment and apology for its past actions, and then develop some policies designed to help reverse those sins of the past—to combat racial alienation and help overcome unemployment, illiteracy, crime and poverty in America's black neighborhoods.

According to statistics from the book *Breaking Down Walls:*

- The 1991 unemployment rate for black Americans was 12.9 percent, more than double the rate for whites.
- Infant mortality is double for blacks what it is for whites.
- In 1990 only 37 percent of black families included both a mother and a father—a figure that has dropped by 41 percent in 30 years.
- More than half of all African-American children are born to single women.
- In the 10 largest urban areas in the U.S., the high school dropout rate for black males is a staggering 72 percent.
- Murder is the leading cause of death for black males between the ages of 15 and 34.
- Blacks account for 44 percent of all murder victims in this country, even though we make up only 12 percent of the population.

Can we ignore statistics like this and pretend that everything is as it should be? Absolutely not! The love of Christ compels us to work for change.

Unfortunately, the Christian community at large has fallen far short of what we could and should do. A 1990 survey undertaken by *Christianity Today* revealed that blacks make up only eight percent of the work force of 24 of America's largest Christian employers. This contrasts with an overall national percentage of fifteen percent. Once again, when Christians should be leading the way, we are lagging behind everyone else.

This is terrible and ought to be cause for mourning. As my son Spencer writes in *More than Equals:*

When the world sneers at our God because we cannot conquer the racial giant, we ought to fall on our knees as Nehemiah did. Unfortunately, instead we usually accept racial separation as much as the world does. *Guilt* has become a dirty word, something we go to therapy to get rid of.

We need to learn how to mourn and grieve because the name of God stands disgraced by our racial problem. It is only as each individual starts with himself or herself, confessing and receiving forgiveness from God, that there will be a basis for racial reconciliation.

If you are ready to admit that there is a real problem in this country, you have taken a big first step toward the elimination of the problem.

2. Confess your own guilt.

If you are a Christian, then you know you are a sinner. The Bible is clear on that point. And I would dare say that if we examine our lives closely enough, most of us can find ways in which we have sinned by perpetuating racial division. These are personal sins that must be dealt with.

Even if a close examination of your life fails to turn up anything, it is still appropriate to confess the guilt of our fathers. For an example of this, see Daniel 9, beginning with verse four:

> And I prayed to the Lord my God, and made confession, and said, "O Lord, great and awesome God, who keeps His covenant and mercy with those who love Him, and with those who keep His commandments, we have sinned and committed iniquity, we have done wickedly and rebelled, even by departing from Your precepts and Your judgments. . . ."

Examine Daniel's life and you will see that he was a righteous man who would never consider disobeying God, not even when threatened with being thrown into a den of lions. Daniel was living at a time when the nation of Judah had been conquered and her people carried away into slavery. What had happened to Judah came as a result of the sins of the people in general—but you can examine Daniel's life with a microscope and you will not find anything he did that contributed to his nation's enslavement. Nevertheless, Daniel realized that what had befallen Judah was the result of sin, and he was willing to bear the burden of that sin.

The same is true of Nehemiah, who wept before God while confessing the sins of his fathers.

You see, there are personal sins and there are societal sins. It is because of societal sins that we have racial strife and violence in this country. Anyone who wants to see our country healed must be willing, as Daniel and Nehemiah were willing, to help shoulder the load of our society's sin.

In her book *Possessing the Gates of the Enemy*, Cindy Jacobs gives an account of something that happened to her friend Dr. Peter Wagner of Fuller Theological Seminary, who was on his way to speak at a conference in Japan:

> Peter was having his morning time of prayer when he began to think about the Japanese people and the pain that they had gone through in Hiroshima and Nagasaki. All of a sudden he started to weep and weep. This puzzled him because he had been only fifteen years old when the bombs were dropped in Japan. He had not participated in the dropping of the bombs nor had he anything to do with the decision to drop the bombs. God showed him, however, that as a fifteen-year-old boy he had hated the Japanese and that there had been fifteen-year-old Japanese boys who were killed during the bombings. Because of his own hatred he was just as guilty as those who had made the decision to drop the bombs. He later realized that in his weeping God had moved him into a time of deep intercession for the nation.
>
> When his wife, Doris, phoned later that morning he shared what had happened. Doris said to him, "Peter, perhaps the Lord would have you repent for Hiroshima and Nagasaki." As soon as Doris spoke the words, Peter knew that this was exactly what the Lord was calling him to do.
>
> Upon arriving in Japan he spoke to the leaders of the conference and asked if they would gather a group of people whose relatives died when the bombs were dropped on Hiroshima or Nagasaki. They were able to do so and arranged a time when he would do what the Lord had told him to do—ask forgiveness publicly for his sin.

When the time came to repent, Peter spent quite a bit of time preparing the people. . . . Just like Daniel he was going to say, "Father, I have sinned." He was not trying to make a judgment as to whether or not the bombs should have been dropped, but rather he wanted to be used by God as an instrument to heal broken, devastated people.

Peter asked those who had lost loved ones when the bombs were dropped to come forward. Then this servant of God knelt to ask forgiveness for his sin and wept big tears asking God to heal the Japanese people. All across the room the Holy Spirit swept into broken hearts, and that room with one thousand people was filled with the sound of weeping—some loud and anguished. The pain of a people was being released and washed away by those tears.

When Peter finished and stood to his feet a Japanese representative rose to speak and declared that their sin as a people was much greater than that of the Americans and asked the Lord to forgive them of their sins against the United States in World War II. Through that experience the Holy Spirit moved into the heart of a nation to bring healing and restoration.

It grieves me that this country has never officially repented of her past sin of slavery. Yes, the slaves were finally set free, but that did not undo all the injustices of the past. As far as I know there has never been an official apology on the part of the U.S. government, nor a day set aside to reflect on those past sins, as well as the continuing sins of racism and racial division. Establishing a day like that, I believe—a day set aside as a national time of racial reconciliation and forgiveness—would be a great step forward in the healing of this country.

But even if that is done, complete healing cannot be brought about by an act or proclamation of the government. It can be accomplished only through individuals—people like you and me.

Are you willing to help bear the burden and shame that racial division has brought to this country? Are you willing to let God break your heart over the sins of our society with regard to slavery and bigotry and men mistreating other men because their skin is either too light or too dark? If you are, then God will honor your attitude and use you as a minister of peace and healing.

Otherwise, it may be true that before you can change anything else, you will have to change yourself. But God is available to help in that, too. If you as a black person think that all whites are arrogant and condescending, spend time praying about it and see if God does not bring someone into your life who is just the opposite—someone who will help you overcome your prejudice.

Since we are already talking about prayer, let's talk about the third thing you must do if you would be an instrument of racial reconciliation:

3. Seek God's guidance.

Prayer is the preparation for ministry, but a lot of Christians have the wrong idea about prayer. They think it is talking to God, while prayer also involves listening to God—listening expectantly for Him to speak to our hearts.

So ask God what He wants you to do, and expect Him to answer you. Ask Him sincerely. And keep on asking until you get His answer. While you are at it, ask Him for the strength and wisdom to accomplish the task He gives you to do.

Let God show you areas in your community where you can be involved in helping to bring about reconciliation. Ask Him to reveal to you areas where you need to grow, or areas where you have a special gift for service. You may not feel much like an expert, but if you are yielded to God, He will use you as a peacemaker. And remember what Christ said: "Blessed are the peacemakers, for they shall be called sons of God" (Matthew 5:9).

4. Be willing to take risks.

It is not easy to be a risk-taker, especially in a world that often seems to give itself over to negativity and hate. But it helps a lot if you remember two things:

Love is stronger than hate.

Light is stronger than darkness.

If you are armed with the love and light of God, there is not an enemy anywhere who can stand against you. And the more risks you take, the stronger and more sure of this you will become.

A risk does not have to be a big thing, something like going into south-central Los Angeles to talk to the Crips and Bloods about Jesus Christ. Certainly that may be a risk God calls you to take, but it is more likely to be something smaller, and in its own way just as significant.

When I talk about taking a risk, I am talking about being willing to be rejected or humiliated in order to build a bridge to someone of another race. Should I try to be your friend, or will you reject me because I am black—or white? If I am afraid of being rejected, I will never take the risk, and the bridge will never get built.

Again, the best advice I can give you about taking risks is to start small. Then, as God gives you more courage and strength, be willing to step out in faith and take risks of greater magnitude.

You should not feel bad if the risks you are taking do not seem to be great. Wherever you are starting, it is a launching pad for bigger and more noteworthy accomplishments in the future. The important thing is to start somewhere.

One good place to start is simply to introduce yourself to someone of another color or ethnic background and try to cultivate a friendship with him or her. In fact, I would have to say that that is a very good place to start, because as I travel around the country, I can see that there is very little social interaction among the races—quite a bit less, in fact, than there was, say, ten years ago.

The Berlin Wall was torn down within the last few years, but the wall of separation between the races in America has grown higher than ever. Risking rejection by saying hello to a member of another race is a good way to start putting some cracks in that wall.

5. Discover opportunities for action.

If you keep your eyes open, you will discover some opportunities for action. After you have prayed about it and made yourself ready to take risks, just walk around your community and talk to people, and you will begin to find out what the needs are.

I really appreciate a story Raleigh Washington tells in *Breaking Down Walls* about an experience he had at an ROTC camp at Fort Benning, Georgia, during his college days. Washington made a white friend there, a young man named Bill Sweet. As he tells the story:

> We'd been doing maneuvers in ninety-degree heat when we took a mid-morning break. I was standing under a shade tree drinking from my canteen when Bill ran up and said, "Raleigh, give me a drink. I forgot my canteen." I reached back to get my cup out of the canteen cover to pour him some water. Bill gave me the strangest look, slapped the cup away, and grabbed the canteen. Then he pulled it straight to his mouth and took a long drink.
>
> *A white man drinking from my canteen!* I can hardly express the feelings that came over me as Bill Sweet drank from my canteen. That was 1959; when we went into town, I had to sit in the back of the bus while he rode in the front. We could not drink from the same water fountain. But he drank from my canteen. Bill was from Charleston, South Carolina, and knew exactly what he was doing. He intentionally used that simple act to break down centuries of alienation between us. Suddenly, I felt the invisible but ever-present walls between us no longer existed.

What Bill Sweet did was not anything great or heroic. But he had seen an opportunity to do something that would help topple the wall of racial separation that stood between him and his friend, and he did not let it pass. It was a little thing, but it meant so much that Washington still vividly recalls the incident more than thirty years later.

How can a white person find opportunities to be an instrument of reconciliation? Here is some good advice from Chris Rice in *More than Equals:*

> If you don't know about black people, begin to learn. . . . Go to a Christian Community Development Association conference and find out what ministries are doing in black communities. Find the black ministries that are working in your area and ask for a tour. Ask how you can serve and volunteer your skills. Start supporting them financially. Visit, or even become a member of, a black church. Start a conversation with a black classmate. If you do not have black students in your campus fellowship, seek out a black Christian student and try to become his or her friend. Hang out in

the black student union. Attend an NAACP meeting. Reach out to a black person at work.

In every community there is a need that only you can fill, and if you do not fill it, the world will be poorer for it. So will you, because you have missed something important. Benjamin Mays, who served for years as president of Morehouse College, often reminded his students of this truth. Many great men and women who came out of that school (including Martin Luther King, Jr.) grabbed the opportunities for service that came their way.

Here are some specific ways you can look for opportunities to be an instrument of reconciliation:

- *Volunteer some time with a ministry that has ongoing outreach to the minority residents of your community.* Generally any ministry reaching out to the poor or the inner city will also be reaching out to minorities, since the majority of the poor in this country are of African or Latin origin. Getting involved with such a ministry will give you a firsthand look at the needs that exist there, as well as a better understanding of what you personally can do about the needs in your community.
- *Build a ministry team.* You can do this by sharing your vision with the people in your home church. Encourage them to join you as you look around your community for opportunities to serve. You will find that excitement, strength and power will flow out of your commitment to one another, as well as your commitment to the common goal of reconciling people across racial, ethnic and economic barriers.
- *Spend time getting prepared.* Once you have built a team of like-minded Christians, you should spend as much time as possible getting together for prayer and fellowship. This is extremely important, for two reasons. First, it will strengthen you in the power of the Holy Spirit, which is something you will definitely need as you move into a ministry of reconciliation. Second, time in prayer and fellowship will help knit you together as a group, building a unity that will not dissolve at the first sign of difficult times or conflict.

- *Choose your target area.* The reason some people give up on the idea of being reconcilers in their community is that they start out too big and soon get discouraged. It is O.K. to start small. Perhaps you want to zero in on an area that is only a few blocks square. Jesus described the Kingdom of God as being like a mustard seed that starts out tiny but grows into a huge tree. Always remember, if you give your efforts to God, He will take your small beginnings and multiply them.
- *Start a Bible study in an inner-city neighborhood.* If at all possible, start the Bible study in someone's home, so that people from the community will feel comfortable about attending. Starting a Bible study is an excellent means of getting to know the residents of the area where you want to work, and of building a Christian base from which to reach into the surrounding community.
- *Work with the neighborhood children.* Let me tell you something I have learned over the years: If you do something good for the children, the parents will like you. Not only like you, but respect and listen to you.

When Vera Mae and I first moved with our children back to California, we started working with a few of the kids in our neighborhood. We made it clear that we were determined to build a better future for the kids of our neighborhood—a neighborhood that had the highest daytime crime rate of any neighborhood in the U.S. That meant providing daycare and Bible clubs for the youngsters. In our case, it also meant putting our lives on the line in order to drive out the drug-dealers and gangsters who were destroying the lives of the kids. Today we work with hundreds of kids every day, and although our neighborhood is far from perfect, it has come a long way from what it was just a few years ago.

Keep your eyes and ears open. Opportunities for service are all around you.

6. Move beyond saying hello.

Merely saying hello to a person of another race or ethnic background is a big step for some people. But it is only the first step. If that is where you leave it, you have not really accomplished very much. It is important for whites, blacks and Hispanics to get to know each other, to engage in serious dialogue. Believe me, that is not always easy. Blacks are often suspicious of whites, and it may take some effort to get beyond that suspicion. Sometimes whites are motivated more by guilt than by a genuine interest in a black person as a human being. That, too, may be difficult to deal with.

O.K., we might as well face it: Sometimes, even though they may not mean to, white people have feelings of superiority that express themselves in a condescending attitude, and that can be a source of friction. Some blacks have these feelings of superiority, too. Or we have feelings of inferiority that push us in the direction of defensiveness, resentment and bitterness. Such attitude problems really get in the way when two people are trying to develop an honest, open friendship and commitment to each other. It may take a lot of love and patience to move beyond saying hello, but it will be worth it.

My son Spencer talks about the differences between friends and "yokefellows," and I think the distinction is important. In the area of multi-racial or multi-cultural relationships, we should all strive to be yokefellows—people who are bound together, committed to each other, who will not desert each other at the first sign of hardship or disagreement.

Here are some of the differences Spencer points out in *More than Equals* between friends and yokefellows:

Friendship can be something that just happens with very little effort, whereas it takes effort to become yokefellows.

Friendships are built for the benefit of the people who are in them, whereas yokefellows pledge themselves to each other for the benefit of God's Kingdom.

Friends are drawn together by their common interests, while yokefellows are drawn together by their common mission—to further the Kingdom of God.

Friends just naturally like each other, while yokefellows put a higher priority on respecting each other.

Friendships are based on compatible personalities; the yokefellow bond is based on gifts that are needed to reach specific goals.

Friendships are based on emotion, while yokefellows are linked together by commitment.

Friends who are separated by a fight or argument may never speak to each other again, but yokefellows will cheer each other on until their common goal is reached.

There you have six things you must do in order to be an instrument of racial reconciliation: *Acknowledge the existence of the problem and the way it affects you; confess your own guilt; seek God's guidance; be willing to take risks; discover opportunities for action;* and *move beyond saying hello.* As you move through these steps, let me give you what I consider to be a very good piece of advice: "Don't take it personally."

If you are a white person reaching out to blacks and other minorities in your community, some folks may call you a nigger-lover, or even worse.

If you are a black person reaching out to whites, some people are going to call you an "Oreo"—you know, black on the outside but white inside—or an Uncle Tom, or something that could never be printed in this book.

When that happens, you need to know that it is their problem, not yours. The racial problems in this country and world will not be solved without a lot of hard work. When I encounter prejudice or a racist attitude, I do not see it as a reaction to my inferiority, and I do my best not to get overly upset about it. Racism is no reflection on me, but on what America is and has been. My job is to work to make it better.

I do not know much about Rodney King, but I certainly liked what he said when he went on television and appealed for calm during the riots, almost pleading for an end to the fighting and bloodshed: "Can't we all get along?"

That question still hangs in the air. Christ's love for all mankind demands that we strive to answer it with a resounding "Yes, we *can* and *will* get along!"

13 Heeding the Call to Reconciliation

Tom Tarrants

What should be a true Christian's response to God's work of reconciliation through Jesus Christ? In a word, *love*—and this has racial implications. When we are converted, God pours His love into our hearts by the Holy Spirit whom He gives us at conversion. This love enables us, for the first time in our lives, to truly love Him and love others. Thus, Jesus could sum up our whole duty to God in terms of loving God and neighbor.

What does it mean to love God? We need to understand that in the Bible loving God is not primarily a matter of feeling or emotion. That is hard for many of us to grasp because we live in a generation preoccupied with subjectivity and feeling; but it is true nonetheless. In Scripture, love for God is a matter of personal devotion, loyalty and faithfulness, expressed primarily through commitment and obedience.

This is not to say that loving God is a colorless, passionless act of willpower. Of course feeling is involved. But commitment, not feeling, is the essence of love. This commitment is manifested in a life that seeks to please God. As Jesus put it, "If you love me, you will obey what I command" (John 14:15). Likewise John wrote, "This is love for God: to obey his commands. And his commands are not burdensome" (1 John 5:3).

The second command God gives us is to love our neighbor as ourselves. Love, we are told, does its neighbor no harm. What is the nature of this love? In modern American church culture we have reduced it to a matter of feeling or sentimentalism. This is a tragic misunderstanding. In the New Testament the Greek word *agape* is the main word for love, and *agape* is not primarily a feeling at all, but rather an act of our wills. Loving others, said William Barclay, is simply choosing to act in their highest and best interests.

Jesus gave us a simple guide when He told us to do for others what we would want them do for us (Matthew 7:12). Obviously love, in order to find expression, requires relationships with other human beings. Most often (but not always, as the story of the Good Samaritan demonstrates) it is when we have a proper relationship with another human being that by our actions we understand how to act in his or her best interest. The bottom line is that by our actions we are to show love to our neighbor—anyone in our life who has need, even across the boundaries of race, ethnicity, culture, social class and friendship. Yes, even our enemies. Through our deeds, Christ's love becomes manifest to them.

Even more is required when it comes to fellow believers. Jesus tells us that we are to love our brothers and sisters as He has loved us, and He goes on to say that we are even to lay down our lives, if need be, for them (John 15:13; 1 John 3:16). For us whites, this includes concern for our black brothers and sisters, from whom we can learn much and who are often in need of help that we could give, if only we would.

How can we love God and others in this way? Not simply out of duty, though that is important; nor out of discipline, though that, too, is important. Rather, we can love God and others out of gratitude to God for all He has done for us in and through Jesus Christ our Lord. Our love for God and obedience to Him must always be the overflow of gratitude from our hearts. When this is so, no sacrifice is too great. Indeed, any sacrifice is a privilege.

As we live a life of love for God and others, we will find ourselves being God's ambassadors of reconciliation. He calls us to work in whatever ways He has gifted and called us to help others find peace with Him. Simply put, this means living as witnesses of the transforming power of Jesus Christ, in two ways—through our verbal testimony as to who Jesus is and what He has done for us, and through the confirming testimony of our own lives lived under His Lordship. When our words and deeds are congruent, people will see Jesus. If our words and deeds are not congruent, we send a mixed message that confuses people and has no credibility.

The American Church has a great credibility problem on account of such incongruence. One of the major areas of sin in which this incongruence is manifested is racial alienation. Unbelievers know that believers are called to love one another and their neighbors. They also know that racial prejudice is not an expression of love. The confession of faith and the simultaneous manifestation of racial alienation amounts to hypocrisy, a charge often heard by those who engage in personal evangelism.

If we love God and want to love others and bring them into His Kingdom, we will want to rid ourselves of our lack of concern and racial prejudice, and engage the world, black and white, with the reconciling love of Jesus Christ.

This is demonstrated clearly in the life of my good friend John Perkins. He is a peacemaker who seeks to reconcile people to God and to one another, and his ministry is motivated by love for God and love for others. May God help each of us to do likewise.

Francis of Assisi, who obeyed the call of Jesus to be a peacemaker (Matthew 5:9), summed it up well: "Lord, make me an instrument of Your peace. Where there is hatred, let me sow love; where there is injury, pardon; where there is discord, unity; where there is doubt, faith; where there is error, truth; where there is despair, hope; where there is sadness, joy; where there is darkness, light. . . ."

This is demonstrated clearly in the life of my good friend John Perkins. He is a peacemaker who seeks to reconcile people to God and to one another, and his ministry is motivated by love for God and love for others. May God help each of us to do likewise.

Practical Principles

Keeping these overarching principles in mind, I want to share with you eleven foundations that I believe are necessary for us to be effective agents of reconciliation. These are not special truths having to do with racial issues, but basic biblical truths that apply to all of life, with particular relevance to racial reconciliation. This list is not complete and my comments are only brief. I trust that others will develop these in greater depth. They are:

1. **Repentance**
2. **Forgiveness**
3. **Patience and Communication**
4. **Humility**
5. **Servanthood**
6. **Unity in Relationships**
7. **Prayer**
8. **Spiritual Warfare**
9. **Faith and Obedience**
10. **Following the Holy Spirit**
11. **Commitment and Sacrifice**

1. Repentance

Repentance is the starting point for racial reconciliation, for both blacks and whites. I do not mean repentance unto salvation. (I assume that the reader has come to a living faith in Jesus Christ through faith and repentance.) What I mean is repentance for particular sins of racial attitudes and behavior, including attitudes of resentment or hatred toward others because of their race; hurtful words and deeds toward others because of their race; and especially attitudes of pride and arrogance because of our own race.

While both blacks and whites have need of such repentance, historically there has been far more racial pride and sin on the part of whites. Whites have held the reins of power in this country since her founding, yet have done little until recently to address the plight of those in the black community. Progress in many instances has been little more than grudging acquiescence to federal court orders and legislation.

Today it seems that white concern may be diminishing rather than increasing. Some whites are reacting against affirmative action. Others feel that blacks have been given plenty of opportunities over the past thirty years and have failed to capitalize on them. Still others feel that blacks are becoming more hostile and belligerent and showing little appreciation for what whites have done to help them. Some are just weary of what they perceive to be an unending stream of black complaints about racism and injustice. To the extent that we whites have allowed these or other thoughts to poison our attitudes toward our black brothers and sisters, we need to examine our thinking in light of God's Word and, where necessary, repent. Even if we do not agree with our black brethren on certain issues, we can still be friends, learn from each other and work together.

Blacks are experiencing growing anger and frustration toward whites. They see us as largely unconcerned with their plight. We are content to live in the comfortable suburbs and enjoy the good life while they continue to be devastated by drugs, poverty, crime, unemployment, poor education and lack of opportunity. These are seen as black problems until there is a riot; then there is an outcry that lasts about as long as a threat seems to exist. Once the danger subsides, things soon return to normal with little change. Many blacks conclude, therefore, that white interest in their situation is motivated largely by fear that things might get out of hand and spread to the suburbs and to our own families.

It is true that blacks have made some gains in recent years. Thanks to civil rights legislation, the twin evils of segregation and discrimination have been abandoned as official public policy (though neither has by any means disappeared). Thanks to improved access to education and employment, the number of black families earning $50,000 a year has grown from 9.9 percent in 1970 to 14.5 percent in 1990. But this must be viewed in light of the fact that, while the black median income for this period grew from $21,151 to $21,423, the white median income for 1990 was $36,915.

Economics is only a small part of the picture, but it is enough to show that life for most blacks is far different than for most whites. The simple fact is, there is a major gap between the races.

There is much truth to the black perspective that many whites *are* unconcerned about the inequities. But blacks who want reconciliation and change need to accept whites, seek to educate them and work with them as equal partners in the struggle.

Although much more could be said, it is clear that whether you are black or white, you must deal with your own attitude before you can work effectively for reconciliation. So long as you are part of the problem, you cannot be part of the solution. Regardless of what others may do, we must get our own hearts right before God. With the help of the Holy Spirit, we must search our hearts and confess and forsake any racial sin, past or present. Then we must follow this up with new attitudes and actions. Professions of concern without principled action are insincere and hypocritical, and there has already been far too much of that.

Why is repentance critical? First of all, because our sinful attitudes grieve God and hinder Him from using us in reconciliation. Second, because getting right with one another is necessary to demonstrate to our brothers and sisters that we are serious about reconciliation. If we cannot recognize and acknowledge our sin up front, how can we take each other seriously on anything else? How can we develop trust in our relationships?

Once we make things right with God and with one another, we are in a position to develop solid relationships, and for God to use us as He sees fit.

2. Forgiveness

Forgiveness and repentance go hand in hand. We will see no real progress between blacks and whites until we forgive one another. Why? Because many hurts are still unresolved.

It goes without saying that American blacks have experienced more unkindness and injustice at the hands of whites than whites have experienced at the hands of blacks. No one can deny that. Whether we talk about the slavery of the past or the racist attitudes and actions of the present, whites have been perpetrators more often than victims. Until we whites understand and admit this, we will make little progress.

White denial, currently and historically, is a major hindrance to reconciliation. And it is doubly hard for blacks to forgive us when we deny our offenses. We need to take the initiative here by recognizing our sins, or at least the sins of our race, and asking for forgiveness.

Many whites feel that if they have done nothing wrong personally to black people, they need not concern themselves with this matter. This overlooks the fact that we are part of a race that for many years overtly oppressed and exploited black people for economic gain, and that the effects of this exploitation continue to be felt to the present day.

Life for most blacks in America today is shaped by the fact that their history in this country began with slavery to white masters. Any people held in slavery suffers not only the degradation of being treated as property but also a profound demoralization of spirit. This historical fact is part of the cultural story passed from generation to generation; it shapes personal identity and expectations. It is also a significant factor in several issues currently affecting African-Americans.

Whites typically respond that blacks have been given plenty of opportunity and have no one to blame but themselves for not "pulling themselves up by their bootstraps," as other immigrants have. Many ethnic groups have come to America from places like Europe, Asia and South America and have eventually taken their place in the mainstream of American life, with all the benefits that brings. But, as Tom Skinner points out, this is comparing apples to oranges, inasmuch as blacks, because of their unique history as American slaves, have faced far more difficult obstacles than European, Asian or Hispanic immigrants.

We whites need to acknowledge, *at the very least,* the racial sin of other whites, express our sorrow over it and our personal repudiation of it. Maybe we can say something like this: "What people of my race have done to people of your race is a sin and a tragedy and I deeply regret it." Daniel and Nehemiah took on the sins of both their contemporaries and their ancestors and repented for them (Daniel 9:4–19; Nehemiah 1:5–7). Should we do less?

On the other hand, can any of us, black or white, say that we are really innocent of sinful racial attitudes? This is such a pervasive sin, as Dr. Sam Hines has observed, that none of us can put ourselves outside its circle.

The need for forgiveness applies not only to issues of the past but to issues that arise in our relationships today. It is inevitable that whites, out of ignorance or insensitivity, will offend blacks. Because we are part of the dominant culture, we have not had to learn the black culture, and few of us know much about it. (Blacks, on the other hand, as the minority race, have had to learn how to understand and adjust to white culture in order to survive.) Thus, when well-meaning whites work with blacks, we make unintentional blunders that hurt or offend our black brothers and sisters.

At that point blacks have two options: to take offense and react in outright anger or quiet withdrawal, or to exercise patience and self-control and use the incident to educate and disciple the white brother into a better understanding of the issues he is blind to, so that he will not repeat his mistake. (Otherwise he *will* repeat it and resentment will build in those offended.) This is the path of love, which is patient and kind.

Sometimes it seems easier and more natural to blow up, but the Bible says that "man's anger does not bring about the righteous life that God desires" (James 1:20). We will never make progress toward reconciliation if we hold onto anger, bitterness and resentment and refuse to forgive and move on.

This is not to say that anger is always wrong. There are matters about which people *should* feel anger and righteous indignation. Jesus certainly did. There are also matters about which the *lack* of moral outrage is a sin. The point is that we not let our anger either eat us up or blow us up. Rather, we should let it energize us to work toward righteous solutions and reconciliation. Regardless of what whites do, blacks need to free themselves from any bondage of resentment by taking the spiritual and moral high ground of forgiveness. If we mean to follow Jesus Christ, we must forgive.

Make no mistake about it, forgiveness is a hard business, especially when you are the one who has been sinned against and those
who have sinned against you do not acknowledge it and ask forgiveness. We have all had times when we were so hurt that we did
not want to forgive. But in light of all that God has forgiven us,
we simply *cannot* withhold forgiveness from those who have
sinned against us. By holding onto unforgiveness, ironically, blacks
keep themselves enslaved to whites—spiritually and emotionally,
if nothing else.

Besides, as Jesus showed us in the parable of the unmerciful servant (Matthew 18:21–35), unforgiveness is not an option. If we do
not forgive, Jesus said, God will not forgive us:

> "Then the master called the servant in. 'You wicked servant,' he
> said, 'I canceled all that debt of yours because you begged me to.
> Shouldn't you have had mercy on your fellow servant just as I had
> on you?' In anger his master turned him over to the jailers until he
> should pay back all he owed. This is how my heavenly Father will
> treat each of you unless you forgive your brother from your heart"
> (Matthew 18:32–35).

These are strong and sobering words—words that illustrate the
overwhelming importance of forgiveness no matter what the
issue.

How can we forgive when it is hard and we do not feel like it?
By remembering that forgiveness is first and foremost a matter
of the will. At heart forgiveness is a choice, a decision to release
another from any claim I may have against him or her. I can
choose to forgive whether I feel like it or not. And as I choose to
forgive by an act of my will, my feelings will eventually come
into alignment.

In some cases forgiveness may be so hard that we need the help
of other believers to counsel and pray us through.

"You gotta love 'em."

John Staggers often used those words, usually when someone
had done something thoughtless or mean and John's friends
thought he should be at least a little bit angry about it. Another
thing he often said, with a smile on his face, was, "You gotta for-

give 'em." And he always did. Sometimes someone would urge John to "shake the dust off your feet" in reference to someone who had done him wrong, but he would say, "Seventy times seven!"

That reply of Jesus to Peter, who had asked Him how many times he had to forgive someone's wrongdoing, indicates that there are no limits to forgiveness. (Seven times, Peter had thought, would be more than generous.)

I have seen both John Staggers and Sam Hines demonstrate love and forgiveness seventy times seven. Those men have loved and forgiven many people right into the Kingdom of God.

One time John and Dr. Hines took three of their staff members on a trip to South Africa. While they were there, they went to a beach to get in a little swimming. There was just one problem—a sign that said *Whites Only*. One of the staff members, who was white, went on into the water to swim, leaving his black colleagues sitting on the shore. He did not do it out of maliciousness; he just did not think about how his brothers would feel.

John waited until a private moment to explain to the young man how his action had hurt the others. He explained in patience and love, accepted the contrite apology that followed and *reaffirmed his love for him*. Then the incident was forgiven and forgotten.

That young man is now serving God effectively in a ministry to poor and homeless black people.

3. Patience and Communication

Situations arise in any relationship that require us to be patient, and our response to these occasions can either make or break the relationship. This is true of marriage, family, friendships and especially interracial friendships. A little patience can be the oil poured on troubled waters.

I have learned a lot about patience from the patience that people like John Staggers, Sam Hines, Tom Skinner and John Perkins have shown me. They have consistently demonstrated kindness, acceptance and longsuffering, even though I have said and done dumb things through ignorance or insensitivity.

Since others have to bear with us, we should do the same with them. This is beautifully expressed by Thomas à Kempis in *The Imitation of Christ:*

> Endeavor to be patient in bearing with the defects and infirmities of others, of what sort soever they be, for that thou thyself also hast many failings which must be borne with by others. If thou canst not make thyself such a one as thou wouldest, how canst thou expect to have another fashioned to thy liking?

We cannot expect people, in other words, to be perfect. Just as God loves and accepts us even when we fail Him, so we must love others patiently even when they fail us. The truth is, it takes most of us a long time to learn things. We often take two steps forward and one step back. But with patient, loving acceptance, we eventually learn and grow.

In order for patience to be worked out in a relationship, each person must be committed to the other. They must also strive to keep the lines of communication open, and be willing to work to resolve conflicts that arise rather than allowing them to fester. We must take special care not to judge the motives of others, because we are often wrong. This is particularly troublesome in black and white relationships. Because of our differing cultural and social experiences, it is easy for persons of either race to misinterpret the true motives of the other.

Dr. Hines offers helpful insight along this line: "The distance between the worlds in which polarized people live makes patience a necessary feature of the journey to reconciliation. The removal of the barrier through God's work at Calvary (Ephesians 2:13–16) does not automatically reduce the distance. Spiritual consciousness and cultural awareness are seldom functioning on the same level."

Patience and communication are particularly important in overcoming the destructive effects of racial stereotyping. People of both races have developed stereotypical ideas of each other. Such stereotypes tend to focus on the negative behavior of a few people and are hardly the basis for accurate perception. We must deal with people as individuals and take the time and effort to build friendships with them. Only in this way can we understand others, recognize their motives and break down our stereotypes of one another.

Open, honest, sensitive communication is an essential ingredient in building such relationships.

John Perkins tells me that he gets frustrated by blacks who always expect the white man to "slip up" and show himself for who he really is. At the first sign of a racist comment or attitude, they are ready to jump all over him, even if it means damaging or destroying a long-term relationship.

We whites need to be patient with our black brothers and sisters and not expect them to think and act just as we do. Our cultures and experiences of life, which influence the way we perceive and react, are much too different for that. We especially need to be patient with the anger and frustration blacks feel over white indifference to the serious problems they face—problems like poverty, drugs, family breakdown and the subtle and not-so-subtle forms of racism that still exist, to name only a few. Sometimes blacks might even vent their anger on those of us who are trying to help, but more than likely it is not meant personally. In such cases we do well to remember that "a gentle answer turns away wrath" (Proverbs 15:1).

Many other differences could be mentioned, but the point is clear enough. In the final analysis, we must make relationships a top priority, and take the time and effort to know each other and work together in love, understanding and patience.

There are now some excellent resources available for those who want to learn how to overcome cultural differences. See *Cross Cultural Conflict*, D. Elmer (IVP); *Ministering Cross-Culturally*, S. G. Lingenfelter and M. K. Mayers (Baker); and *More than Equals*, S. Perkins and C. Rice (IVP).

4. Humility

Humility is an extraordinarily important virtue for every believer to cultivate. Without it we cannot experience closeness with God, nor can we know the power of the Holy Spirit in our lives and ministries. The reason for this is simple: "God opposes the proud but gives grace to the humble" (1 Peter 5:5).

What is humility? As John Wesley aptly said, it is nothing more than a right view of ourselves. In relation to God, this means a personal awakening to our own frailty, weakness and limits as creatures of an infinite, almighty, holy God. Humility, wrote Andrew Murray in his book of that title, "is simply a sense of entire nothingness, which comes when we see how truly God is all, and in which we make way for God to be all."

In relation to others, humility means making ourselves of no reputation, in order that we may serve Christ in them. This involves seeing others as more important than ourselves and as worthy of our care and service; putting their interests ahead of our own and seeking their good.

For many of us this is hard. As Sam Hines has noted, "Humility is hard for powerful people. It is easier to humiliate than to be humble. The desire to be on top, to get ahead, to tower over, can corrupt aspiration and pollute ambition. People who are driven by the market find humility at least as inconvenient, in a world that demands aggressiveness, as the way toward success." Sadly, this is the case not only in the world, but too often in the Church and with her leaders.

The opposite of humility is pride, which, along with unbelief, is the mother of all sin. Pride seems to have had its origin in the heart of Satan and was the cause of his fall. It was also the basis of his strategy to corrupt Adam and Eve in the Garden of Eden. First he sought to make them dissatisfied with who they were and suggested that God was withholding something good from them. Then he encouraged their unbelief by questioning God's word: "Did God *really* say you would die if you ate from the tree?" Finally he appealed to their pride by telling them they would be as God if they ate the fruit.

Satan has used pride with great effectiveness since that time, and is using a variation of it today to alienate the races. With whites it takes the form of attitudes of racial superiority and arrogance. Hitler's Aryan supremacy is probably the best-known and most virulent expression of racial pride in this century. Next would be the racism of the Ku Klux Klan and kindred groups in America.

We must not make the mistake, however, of thinking that racial pride is limited only to such extremes as these. Although we do not want to admit it, many white people assume themselves (either consciously or unconsciously) to be superior to blacks. They may believe that white culture is superior, or that white social norms are superior, or that they themselves are superior due to genetic makeup. They may focus on the achievements of white European or American culture or on their own accomplishments, seeing them as evidence of innate white superiority.

There is nothing inherently wrong with white or black awareness of their personal achievements or those of their race. Indeed, each race and culture and individual has achievements that can be pointed to with pleasure. The problem comes when those achievements are viewed as proof of one's superiority over other cultures or races or individuals. All our distinctives are gifts from God and must never become the source of pride over others, or they will breed arrogance, division and injustice.

One of the insidious things about pride is that it is difficult to see in oneself. But it surfaces in our relationships with others in the form of attitudes and actions, and a sense of racial superiority is one place where we can begin to deal with it.

Until recently, I suspect, many blacks also believed the myth of white superiority. In recent years, however, they have been awakening to a sense of due appreciation of their own race, which is healthy and productive. Unfortunately, there are those who now boast of black superiority, dismissing whites as "icemen." Ultimately this will cause blacks to reap the same kind of suffering whites have reaped for their racial pride.

Our great need, whether black or white, is to humble ourselves—to recognize our own nothingness in light of the majesty and glory of the God who created all things, seen and unseen. We must ask Him to search our hearts and reveal to us any attitudes of racial or personal superiority that we may hold toward others. We do well to remember what Mother Teresa said: "God works best with nothing." He also works best with nobodies. In the Bible and Church history we see over and over that God uses the nobodies of this world to accomplish His purposes, so that the glory goes to Him alone. As a friend once told me, "God will use any old pipe that is open on both ends."

To put it another way, humility is the grease that lubricates human relationships and makes them healthy and long-lasting.

5. Servanthood

Servanthood is humility in action. Jesus, the Suffering Servant, calls us to follow in His steps and become a servant to others. Nowhere is this more important than in racial reconciliation.

This is a hard lesson to learn, however, a hard attitude to develop. Even among Jesus' first disciples, the impulse to be first and to rule over others was strong. James and John, like many of us today, preferred to rule rather than serve, and sought the highest positions they could get in the coming Kingdom. Their attitude and maneuvering created resentment in their co-laborers.

Scripture and experience teach us that selfish ambition always leads to strife, disunity and division. This is demonstrated, sadly, in all too many churches and ministries today.

What can we do to prevent it? The night that He was betrayed to suffering and death, our Lord Jesus took a towel and washed the feet of His disciples, seeking to impress on them the still-unlearned lesson of servanthood. "Now that you know these things," He told them, "you will be blessed *if you do them.*" (John 13:17, emphasis added). It is not enough to know our need to be a servant; we must take action to become a servant.

This is the same challenge we face today in racial reconciliation. Each of us must make a settled decision to become a servant of our brothers and sisters, and use our gifts and abilities to help them achieve important goals for themselves, for Christ and for His Kingdom.

For whites involved in the work of reconciliation, it means going into the black community as listeners and learners, to serve black leadership. This is an important principle that few whites (at least initially) seem to be aware of. Because we often have the advantage of a good education and a knowledge of how the system works, it is natural for us to bring with us an attitude of knowing just what to do—as if to say, "Fear not; all will be well.

I have arrived!" This can easily give our black brothers and sisters the impression, like the white bwana-ignorant native motif, that we think they know nothing and have no ideas or solutions to contribute.

It often turns out, in fact, that the people we are trying to assist have already thought through and discarded as unworkable our proposed solutions. Their firsthand knowledge of their culture and the dynamics of the problems they face give them a perspective that may not be readily apparent to us whites.

As a matter of wisdom and respect, then, we need to seek insight and understanding from our black brothers and sisters. This comes naturally by serving and observing. Later, as relationships grow stronger, we might ask: "What do you make of this problem? Would you help me understand it from your perspective? What has been done in the past? What do you think needs to be done about it now? How do you think I can best help?"

One of the perennial problems blacks face is well-meaning whites who want to help but are unaware of all the problematic cultural attitudes they bring with them. It is hard when people want to help but unintentionally do as much harm as good. It is also hard for blacks to tell whites about this, which can build up frustration and anger manifested in angry outbursts or silent withdrawal. In either case the relationship will suffer serious if not destructive strain.

For that reason it is easy for blacks to develop the attitude of "Beware, the helping hand strikes again!" It is not uncommon for them to feel they have been burned by whites and that they must proceed with extreme caution. So we need to be patient and take the time for our motives to be made manifest. Also, if we hope to serve our black brothers and sisters, we must learn to recognize and respect their leadership, instead of seeking ownership and control. If we accomplish anything, it will be out of relationships of respect and partnership with black leadership, not in self-sufficient isolation.

Our tendency, I think, is to develop a plan and then ask black leaders to support it. What we should do is form our plans with our black brothers and sisters from the beginning as equal partners in deciding what to do and how to go about it.

A good example of this is Billy Graham's work with black church leaders in a Washington-area crusade during the late 1980s. Far in advance of the crusade, he came to Washington to develop relationships with the black pastors of the city. Out of several meetings with these pastors, some of whom opposed him, friendship and trust developed, laying the foundation for a successful city-wide crusade.

Another example is Dr. Myron Augsburger, founding pastor of Washington Community Fellowship, now a thriving congregation of about four hundred people. Myron is a man of many abilities—a rare combination of scholar and theologian who is also a powerful evangelist. In the late '70s, not long after leaving the presidency of Eastern Mennonite College and Seminary, Myron felt God might be calling him to Washington to establish a church on Capitol Hill.

One of the first things he did was meet with John Staggers and Sam Hines to ask their thoughts about the need for such a church, and how to relate to and reach out to the black community. He knew that the population of Washington was predominantly black, and that Staggers and Hines were highly respected black leaders in the city. As much knowledge and ability as he had, he also knew he had much to learn, and took the path of humility and servanthood.

As a result, he developed some lasting friendships, with respect and trust, and has had an effective ministry in Washington over the years.

Yet another example of humility and servanthood was demonstrated by a wealthy white businessman who for several years personally funded the program of the Third Street Church of God to feed the homeless and poor. This man also came down weekly to help cook and serve the food. None of those working alongside him knew he was paying for all the food. He did not come into the situation throwing his money around or thinking he had all the answers. He came in a spirit of humility and servanthood, and did a tremendous amount of good.

This is an example of the kind of servants we need to become if we are to help bring racial healing.

6. Unity in Relationships

Unity is one of the great keys to the advance of God's Kingdom. By unity I do not mean uniformity, but rather oneness of mind and heart that comes only through our being in Christ and "[submitting] to one another out of reverence for Christ" (Ephesians 5:21). To have unity does not mean I have to think exactly as you think on every issue. It does mean I have to love and respect you as my brother or sister. It also means that we agree to resolve our problems with each other rather than walk away from the relationship and break our unity in Christ.

Unity in the essentials, liberty in the non-essentials and love in everything should be our credo—not only in doctrinal matters but in personal ones as well. If we are serious about spreading the Gospel, we have to be serious about unity, which means we have to be serious about reconciliation. The world should be able to look at believers and see that we are truly one, as Jesus prayed for us to be. Jesus said that our unity will be a sign to the world of His Lordship (John 17:20–23). Our unity is the most effective evangelistic witness. Says Sam Hines, "It is a supernatural, supra-cultural, supra-racial, supra-natural evidence of grace. Is it any wonder that Satan is always sowing division, mistrust and disunity?"

I am reminded again of Sam Hines and John Staggers. Many times I have seen them reach out to embrace those who were different from them—different in politics, race and attitude—and find a common ground on which unity could be built. "If you want to change people," John always said, "you cannot leave them surrounded by those who are just like them." Take the initiative, in other words. Reach out to the people who are different from you and get to know them, trusting that God will work through your relationship to bring about spiritual growth in them . . . and in you!

What we sometimes fail to realize is that people seldom change because of our strident rhetoric, while they often change by seeing things from the perspective of friends they trust. Just as a little seasoning can significantly change the taste of food, so one committed relationship can powerfully alter a life.

Unity across racial lines is a radical witness to the power of Jesus Christ. It gets the attention of people in ways nothing else can. It gives credibility to any effort and is essential if whites are to be effective in ministry with blacks. And last but not least, it is essential for God's blessing to be fully released.

7. Prayer

Attempting to do ministry of any kind apart from a life of serious prayer is not only unspiritual, it is unwise, unhealthy and of limited value. This is especially true in seeking racial reconciliation. Some believers, especially those of us who tend to be activists, may think this is wrong. "There are massive problems out there that need immediate attention," they reason. "We don't have time to pray. We need to get to work!" Others see prayer as a pietistic cop-out, a substitute for action.

While there is no question that the problems facing us are massive, and while there are those who pray rather than act, prayer is fundamental to any effective work of God. Prayer is not the only thing we do, but it is the first thing we do. The Bible, Church history and personal experience show clearly that the ministries that accomplish the most for Christ are the ones that take prayer seriously.

Jesus must be our example in this and Jesus was a man of prayer. In the midst of a busy and fruitful ministry—a ministry that would last for only three years—Jesus often withdrew from the crowds for time alone in prayer (Luke 5:15–16). He knew the necessity of constant communion with the Father. If the Son of God needed to do this in His ministry, how much more do we! I am convinced that one of the reasons Jesus was able to accomplish His mission in just three years of active ministry is that He had cultivated the habit of prayer, communicating with His Father and doing only the things He saw His Father do (John 5:19, 30.)

The truth is, we cannot afford *not* to pray. If we are too busy to pray, we are too busy. It is easy in our society to get into a pattern of responding to the urgent rather than the truly important. But this is a sure road to trouble. Life is too short to waste it trying to minister by our own wit and wisdom and strength. Anyone who does this will eventually burn out and become another casualty.

This is not uncommon, incidentally, among those who work in urban areas. Often they are motivated by guilt or a sense of heroic idealism, which facilitates burnout. Far from being examples of self-sacrifice for the Lord, these are cases of self-sabotage that harm His work by rendering the workers useless and discouraging others from pursuing the ministry.

Each of us needs to maintain a vital daily prayer life—not as a legalistic ritual, still less as a means of getting God to cooperate with our plans, but as vital communication and fellowship with Him. Prayer does not get God to bless our plans; it gets us in touch with Him and His plans—plans He will bless because they are His own. This is where ministry can get really exciting and fruitful.

We also need to pray with others who share our concerns for ministry. Corporate prayer is a proven means of advancing the work of God, as we see clearly in the book of Acts (4:23–31; 12:5ff.). In corporate prayer, strategic direction is often given and the power of the Spirit released (see Acts 13:1–3).

For several years I have been gathering with a group of fifty to sixty men and women to pray for the city of Washington. Originally there were two prayer meetings. One, led by John Staggers and Sam Hines, met at Shiloh Baptist Church and was mostly black. The other, led by Congressman Tony Hall, met at the Martin Luther King Library and was mostly white. Then, after John's death, Sam and Tony got together and were led to merge the two meetings as a witness to reconciliation in the city. I can say, having been involved in both, that the combined meeting is *much* more powerful than either one was before they merged.

We have seen some effective ministries emerge from our group.

This meeting has also been a rallying point for believers concerned about Washington and has been a catalyst for positive changes here. During one period a couple of years ago, we felt moved to pray for the terrible drug problem that was plaguing the city and causing many murders in the black community. Some weeks later the leading drug trafficker in the city was arrested and his entire ring put out of business. I could give other examples.

Another benefit of our weekly prayer meeting has been that it has brought people from different backgrounds together and forged a bond of unity between us. The group is divided about equally between black and white members, with some Hispanics involved as well. And as we have prayed together, we have learned to love one another and to have a common vision for Christ to be glorified in our nation's captial.

Prayer does that. It strips away our defenses and pretenses. When you hear your brothers and sisters pouring out the concerns of their hearts to God, you cannot help but be drawn closer to them and to stand with them. Eventually a deep bond of unity and shared vision will emerge.

8. Spiritual Warfare

What does Paul mean when he tells us that "our struggle is not against flesh and blood, but against the rulers, against the authorities, against the powers of this dark world and against the spiritual forces of evil in the heavenly realms" (Ephesians 6:12)? It means that a war is raging throughout the universe—not a war of words or bullets, but a spiritual war. God and His angels are arrayed against Satan and his demonic hordes, and a pitched battle is being waged unseen by human eyes.

Though the Bible teaches this clearly, in Ephesians and elsewhere, it is hard for most of us to take it seriously. Our Western world view, very different from the biblical world view, is a large part of the problem. Although we acknowledge the reality of the transcendent, we live as if it did not have a tangible effect on the world in which we live and work. Few of us in the Church, sad to say, understand how this cosmic war relates to daily life. Many of us live highly secularized lives with little awareness of the supernatural and even less expectation that it will interrupt our orderly existence. Not really knowing why, we find it difficult to believe that angels and demons are active in world affairs or in our own lives.

But whether we take it seriously or not, the battle rages on.

In his introduction to *The Screwtape Letters,* C. S. Lewis remarked that

> there are two equal and opposite errors into which our race can fall about the devils. One is to disbelieve in their existence. The other

is to believe, and to feel an unhealthy and excessive interest in them. They themselves are equally pleased by both errors and hail a materialist or a magician with the same delight.

We see this in America today. On the one side are those in the Church who are so preoccupied with the cognitive and rational aspects of the faith that they live as if the devil did not exist; and on the other side are those who see a demon behind every teapot that boils over.

Nonetheless, evil spirits actively seek to engender alienation, division and strife in this world—not only between individuals, but between nations, ethnic and racial groups.

By no means is this the only or even the most important dimension of the racial problems we face. It would be simplistic and foolish to blame the devil and his demonic hosts for everything. It would also be a convenient cop-out excusing us from facing the real causes that are rooted in sinful human attitudes and behavior, and excusing us from the hard work of personal reconciliation needed to address the issues. But this must not blind us to the fact that evil spirits are a significant aspect of what we are dealing with.

These evil spirits are unquestionably at work in the arena of racial relationships, seeking to exploit very real problems and injustices in order to fan the flames of division and anger that will lead to violence. It takes little imagination to realize that the devil would like nothing better than to see more of the riots that swept through Los Angeles during the spring of 1992, and a further breakdown of relationships among Christians of different colors. This kind of hatred, suspicion and disunity would damage the cause of Jesus Christ and the witness of the Church in America and the world.

Missions history tells us of tremendous gains made by missionaries after they became involved in spiritual warfare—that is, fasting, intercessory prayer and actively resisting demonic forces in the name of Jesus. The Ku Klux Klan is significantly influenced by demonic forces, although it attempts to wrap itself in the banner of Christianity. I believe that spiritual warfare helped to break up the Klan in Mississippi.

On a personal note, I believe that my own conversion to Christ was due to the prayers of a group of women led by Joyce Watts (the wife of FBI agent Frank Watts) that prayed for me for two years, even while I was in prison plotting ways to commit more violence.

Anyone who moves into the area of racial reconciliation, especially in the inner city, needs to be aware that they will encounter resistance from the forces of darkness. Satan *will* oppose you. This is why you need to learn how to fast, pray and actively resist the powers of darkness. Richard Lovelace's excellent book *The Dynamics of Spiritual Life* discusses this subject in a sane, biblical way and is helpful for a general understanding of this area.

In practical terms, resistance to the work of the devil in race relations will focus to a great extent on fasting and Spirit-led prayer that address critical issues. "Those who neglect prayer in this area," says Sam Hines, "approaching reconciliation as a human enterprise and drawing on their own skills and strategies, will only find them inadequate. To pray is to acknowledge God and His sovereignty in these matters, and to confess our dependence on Him and His resources. Prayer is not abdication of responsibility but the acquisition of unlimited resources."

9. Faith and Obedience

If we are to venture with God rather than operate by our own strength, we must learn to walk by faith. Unfortunately, many of us evangelicals are not willing to go any farther than we can see by the light of our own rationality, our own headlights. As a result, our lives and ministries bear the mark of the earth instead of heaven. All we know to do is walk by sight; it is frightening to think of leaving our comfort zones and learning to walk by faith. Yet this is the call of God to all His children.

What do I mean by faith? Our conception of faith is often a combination of optimism, pragmatism and Yankee ingenuity. But this is not biblical faith. Biblical faith is confidence in God and His loving faithfulness toward us, joined with steps of trusting obedience. The writer of Hebrews put it this way: "Faith is being sure of what we hope for and certain of what we do not see" (11:1). The most basic expression of faith, of course, is belief in the existence of God even though we cannot see Him. Likewise, faith is belief that a Galilean carpenter-turned-wandering-teacher, Jesus of Nazareth, was the Son of God, and that through His death on the cross and His resurrection from the grave, God has opened a way for men and women to be reconciled to Him.

But faith does not end with these fundamental areas of salvation. Faith relates to daily life and ministry. God told Noah, for example, to build a huge ship on dry land. To the onlooking world this surely appeared to be the height of folly. Judged by the standards of a rational ethic, it was indeed foolish, even irrational. But Noah knew and trusted God and was ready to appear foolish to others, if only he might be found faithful and pleasing to God.

The same is true with Abraham. God promised him a child when he and Sarah were far past their fertile years. Abraham knew that siring a child at age 100 was impossible, but this did not weaken his faith because he knew God and was persuaded that God had the power to do what He had promised (Romans 4:18–21).

Noah and Abraham are just two examples God gives us as patterns for our own lives.

Let's look at two areas in which faith is relevant to the ministry of racial reconciliation. First is the fact that the task appears to be impossible. People are quick to say that addressing this long-standing problem is so massive, so complicated, so fraught with tensions, misunderstandings, mistrust and ill will that no progress is possible. But that is all beside the point. The same could be said of many things God has done throughout history.

Nothing was less likely or more formidable than delivering the Hebrew slaves from their Egyptian masters who controlled the most powerful empire in the world. The question is: What does God want in the situation? Once that point is clear we may proceed, assured that what God wants He has the power to accomplish, and no one can thwart Him. When it comes to the reconciliation of believers across racial, social, cultural and ethnic boundaries, the Bible is clear.

The first point of faith, then, is to believe what the Bible shows us to be God's will on this matter, and be willing to play whatever part He has for us.

The second point of faith is to actively seek God's guidance about what we are to do. This will vary, of course, from person to person. On the most basic level, every believer is called to be a peacemaker (Matthew 5:9) and should exercise that role in every arena of his or her life. (Surely peacemaking has some racial dimension!) Other believers are called to a specific, full-time ministry of promoting racial reconciliation. It is not our place to decide what our level of involvement will be; that is for God to show us. And He will, as we earnestly pray for His direction with the intention of obeying whatever He shows us. Once the vision is clear, we must step out in confidence, determined to persevere in the face of any interference or opposition that may come.

Does this sound risky? It is. Someone has well said, faith is spelled *r-i-s-k*. Any personal dealing with God is risky, because His ideas and His will may differ from ours.

Is it dangerous? In some cases it may be. But if God is with us, we need not fear. Our greatest threat is not danger but fear. Fear destroys faith and renders us unable to draw on God's resources. As Clarence Jordan put it in *The Substance of Faith and Other Cotton-Patch Sermons*, "Fear is the polio of the soul which prevents us from walking in faith."

Although God will never ask us to do anything immoral or contrary to His Word, sometimes He may ask us to do things that do not seem to make sense at the time, just as He asked Noah to build the ark, or Abraham to sacrifice Isaac, or Jesus invited Peter to get out of the boat and walk on the water. At such a point we have a decision to make: Will we respond with rationalizations and fear, or with faith and obedience? If we choose the obedience of faith, we can be sure that whatever God calls us to do, He will enable us to accomplish.

10. Following the Holy Spirit

The Holy Spirit is the Spirit of missions. When we are living in the fullness of the Spirit, He not only leads us into ministry but empowers us to do it. That mission, if the book of Acts is any guide, is likely to cross racial, social, ethnic and cultural barriers. We need go no further than Philip's evangelism among the much-despised Samaritans, or Peter's ministry to Cornelius and the Gentiles, or the multi-cultural churches at Antioch and Rome, to see this impulse in action. (It is interesting that none of these situations seems to have been the result of planning.)

The earliest believers were Jews who were quite comfortable in their ethnicity and had no desire to mix with people of other races and cultures. The Holy Spirit had to thrust them into this. But once He did, they recognized God's wisdom and pursued His plan.

My present ministry in the city of Washington, D.C., came about as a result of some unexpected guidance from the Holy Spirit, and has taken me on a similar multi-cultural path.

My wife and I had for many months been seeking God's direction in ministry, believing that God's will for us was to wait until He had opened a definite door. As the months wore on, I am sure family and friends began to wonder if we had lost our common sense. At last, however, we were invited to consider teaching with an international missions organization. As part of the process we attended a five-month initial training program. We thought surely this was what God had been preparing us for.

But while we were in the program, one of the teachers, who had never seen me before and knew nothing about me, shared a message God had put on his heart for me: "Seek the peace and prosperity of the city to which I have carried you into exile" (Jeremiah 29:7).

As he continued to speak, revealing aspects of our lives he had no way of knowing, Charlotte and I knew God was showing us the path we had long sought in prayer.

Responding to this guidance took us in a direction very different from what we anticipated. But God knew what He was doing, and time has proven that we are exactly where we were meant to be. Because of that I have peace and joy, and can labor in the strength and confidence that come only from being in God's will.

This was one of the secrets of John Staggers' life. John always followed the Holy Spirit's leading, no matter what others might say. If the Spirit said, "I want you to reach out to this or that person," he did it. As a result, he found himself in many unusual and sometimes uncomfortable situations, such as close friendships with gang leaders and drug lords, or really strange characters like Chuck Colson, Ollie North, Tom Tarrants and Sidney Davis, a lifer at Lorton Prison who is now a leader in the Cities and Schools organization. But in each case he made a contribution to our lives for Jesus Christ!

Only by allowing the Holy Spirit to fill and lead us can we know what God wants us to do and receive the strength to carry it out. Scripture tells us that every Christian has the Holy Spirit in his or her life by virtue of the new birth. In fact, Paul tells us that if we do not have the Spirit, we are not Christians at all (Romans 8:9).

But not every Christian is filled with the Spirit or under the Spirit's control. Paul commanded the Ephesian believers who had already received the Spirit at conversion (Ephesians 1:13) to be filled with the Spirit. From this one example (there are others), it is clear that to be born of the Spirit does not necessarily mean that we are living in the Spirit's fullness. Equally clear is the fact that God wants us to live daily in a state of fullness.

"Do not get drunk on wine," Paul wrote, "which leads to debauchery. Instead, be filled with the Spirit" (Ephesians 5:18). A more literal translation of this last phrase would be this: "Be ye being filled"—that is, "Be continuously filled with the Spirit." In order to be continuously filled with the Holy Spirit, we have to be yielded and obedient. Only thus can we live and witness effectively for Christ. And only thus can the gifts of the Spirit be manifested fully through us.

God gives each of us certain gifts through the Holy Spirit that are means by which we can manifest His many-sided grace and be a blessing to other believers. As we recognize and use His gifts, we can do much good for His Kingdom. Regardless of one's view of spiritual gifts, every believer should earnestly ask God to furnish him with those gifts that will best enable him to serve others and glorify Christ in his life.

The question for each of us is not "Are you a Pentecostal or charismatic or evangelical or fundamentalist?" but "Are you filled with the Holy Spirit?" If you are filled with the Spirit, you have the power to be an effective witness for Jesus and the ability to help reconcile people to God and to one another. Whether we are fundamentalist, evangelical, charismatic or Pentecostal is beside the point. Our duty is to seek God and be filled with His Spirit daily in order that we might enjoy the presence of Christ, have the mind of Christ, manifest the character of Christ and advance the cause of Christ.

Amen!

As we live and walk by the Spirit, God will give us wisdom and guidance that will help us break through the problems, difficulties and challenges we will face in seeking racial reconciliation. He will also give us boldness to overcome the fear of man and the yearning for acceptance and security that can easily hinder us from faithful obedience.

11. Commitment and Sacrifice

This is the point at which we must come to the bottom line. We have both good news and bad news. The bad news is that following Jesus Christ faithfully carries a cost. The good news is that it is more than worth it. Unlike many today who seek to make Christianity as easy as possible, Jesus was ruthlessly honest with people about what it meant to follow Him. "If anyone would come after me," He said, "he must deny himself and take up his cross and follow me" (Matthew 16:24). What did Jesus mean by this? To answer that question, it helps to understand what those words meant to His original hearers. Let's look at each of the three phrases.

First, when Jesus said that a person *must deny himself,* He meant something very different from what we commonly mean by that phrase today. As F. F. Bruce wrote in *The Hard Sayings of Jesus:* "This phrase has become unconscionably weakened in pious phraseology. Denying oneself is not a matter of giving up something, whether for Lent or the whole of life. It is a decisive saying no to oneself—to one's hopes, plans and ambitions, to our likes and dislikes, to our nearest and dearest—for the sake of Christ." This flies in the face of contemporary, self-absorbed American culture, but it is what Jesus meant His disciples to understand, and that includes us.

Taking up one's cross is another phrase we have trivialized in modern times. Again Bruce tells us that "the sign of a man being taken to the place of public execution was not unfamiliar in the Roman world of that day. Such a man was commonly made to carry the cross-beam—the patibulum—of his cross as he went to his death. This was the picture which Jesus' words would conjure up in the minds of his hearers." The idea is clear: We must be prepared to give up even our lives, if necessary, for Christ.

Finally, Jesus said that one must *follow Him*. By this He meant simply that a person needs to pattern his or her life after His. What characterized Jesus' life? First, a loving devotion to God expressed in radical obedience, humility and servanthood. Second, a love for human beings manifested in an unconquerable benevolence and a commitment to seek their highest good, even at the cost of His own life.

The history of God's people offers many inspiring examples of men and women who took these words of Christ seriously, people who were willing to give all for Him, and in so doing made a major impact on the world. They understood that it was not how long one lives that matters most, but *how* one lives. They were prepared to be faithful even unto death, and as a result they were free to live life to the fullest for Christ and do great exploits for Him, regardless of the consequences.

Self-sacrifice is a natural outgrowth of being reconciled to God. Paul wrote that Jesus died on the cross "that those who live should no longer live for themselves but for him who died for them and was raised again" (2 Corinthians 5:15). Once we understand what Jesus has done for us, once our lives have been changed by His love, what else can we do but give ourselves fully to Him for His purposes?

As Paul wrote in Romans 12:1: "Therefore, I urge you, brothers, in view of God's mercy, to offer your bodies as living sacrifices, holy and pleasing to God—which is your spiritual worship." This was a key principle with John Staggers, who often emphasized that offering our bodies as living sacrifices was our reasonable response to God's love. To those who came to the inner city to work among the poor, John would say, "You're not here to help the poor. You're not here to help the nobodies. You're here to offer up an act of worship to Jesus Christ."

Every follower of Jesus Christ must come to the place of relinquishing everything to God's control—life, family, possessions, reputation, relationships, *everything*. For many of us this seems too high a price to pay. We have become so addicted to ease, comfort, pleasure and security that we find it difficult to hear the call of Jesus. But is the cost really too high? C. T. Studd, the great English missionary, said, "If Jesus Christ be God and gave His life on the cross for me, then no sacrifice that I can make will be too great for Him."

When seen in the light of Christ and of eternity, the cost is not too great. But we will not know that for sure until we stand before Him face to face, and then it will be too late. Perhaps Jim Elliot summed up the issue as succinctly as anyone when he wrote, "He is no fool who gives up what he cannot keep to gain what he cannot lose." That is the issue that confronts this generation.

As you finish this book, know that "the eyes of the LORD range throughout the earth to strengthen those whose hearts are fully committed to him" (2 Chronicles 16:9). Will you trust that Christ is true, that He alone is sufficient for all your need and that He will be faithful to you? Will you abandon yourself to Him recklessly for His purposes in the world today? As someone has written, "We have all eternity to enjoy our victories, but only a few brief moments before the sunset to win them." Now, not tomorrow, is the time to give all to Christ. Will you?

I am, as I said at the beginning of chapter 11, still very much a learner in racial reconciliation. What I have written here represents not a political or ideological viewpoint but my present understanding of a biblical, Kingdom-of-God perspective on this difficult issue. God's perspective is what each of us must seek to discover, since ultimately nothing else matters. And from His perspective we must critique our political, social and racial views. God's Word and God's truth must always stand over and correct our thinking.

I encourage you to search the Scriptures daily to see if these things be true. If they are, embrace them with all your heart and live them out daily for the honor and glory of Jesus Christ.

Amen!

Relearning the Three R's

14

John Perkins

So far Tom and I have given some general ways every one of us can work toward bringing about reconciliation between the races. Some of you reading this book may be called to undertake extraordinary measures. I want to talk specifically to you now about the three R's.

No, not reading, 'riting and 'rithmetic. I am referring to

1. Relocation
2. Reconciliation
3. Redistribution

Let's look at each of these in turn.

1. Relocation

What do I mean by relocation? Exactly what it sounds like: for a white Christian to make the decision to move into a predominantly black or Hispanic community.

It may also mean for a black Christian to leave his own comfort zone and move into a predominantly white neighborhood. But when I think of relocation, I picture it as whites moving into a black neighborhood, since that generally involves a lowering of economic standards rather than a raising of them. Many blacks would gladly move into a more affluent white suburb, while not many middle-class or wealthy whites are interested in moving into the inner city.

I understand that relocation is a hard thing to do. It was hard for me to move my family into the crime-ridden neighborhood of northwest Pasadena, but I knew it was where God wanted us to be.

I am also sure it was terribly difficult for Jesus Christ to leave His home in heaven and come down to earth to be born in a barn. Think about it! That was relocation in its purest sense. Jesus came down here to live among us, work alongside us and experience all the aches and pains of life just as we experience them, so He could do an even better job of showing us how to deal with them—and ultimately bear the penalty for sin on our behalf. How could anyone not love a God like that, a God who, rather than sitting back and watching from a distance, got right down here into the dirt with us?

In the same way, you can become the physical presence of Christ in a poor black or Hispanic community.

In my book *With Justice for All* I put it this way:

But you ask, "Can't a suburban Christian minister to those who are aching without becoming one with them?"

And I answer, "Why on earth do you suppose these people have a welfare mentality?" It is because outside "experts" have come up with programs that have retarded and dehumanized them. Yes, our best attempts to reach people from the outside will patronize them. Our best attempts will psychologically and socially damage them. We must live among them. We must become one with them. Their needs must become our needs.

The decision to relocate is a big decision, a decision to be made only in obedience to God's call. Relocation is not simple. It involves much more than moving to a different house. It requires careful preparation and a clear understanding of how to proceed after the move. And although each ministry will be uniquely shaped around both the gifts of the ministry team and the needs of the community, this basic strategy, with only slight variations, can guide the relocation process wherever it takes place.

What is a white person doing by choosing to relocate in a poor black or Hispanic community? He or she is showing forth the love of God in an obvious and practical way—and I believe that is vitally important. The world needs to hear the Gospel, but it is just as important for the world to see the Gospel in action. It is important for you to accept Jesus as your Savior, but it is just as important for you to accept Him as Lord and do as He directs. And sometimes He directs you and me to take a few giant steps in the direction of self-sacrifice so that other folks will see His love in and through us.

Some people think that preaching the Gospel is coming in and condemning everyone—and that is simply not so. The Gospel is the love of God, the righteousness of God, God's care for humanity. The Gospel is God's concern for His physical creation, too, which is reproducing and bringing forth fruit just as He commanded it to. But some people hoard what it produces and refuse to allow it to be passed on to the poor in our society.

Jesus Christ told His followers that He was the light of the world, and that they were to be the light of the world. I have always believed that the deeper the darkness, the more powerful and visible the light shining in that darkness. If you take a flashlight outside on a bright, sunny day, it will be hard to tell if it is on. The light simply blends in with all the light shining down from the sun. But take that same flashlight inside. Close all the doors, pull the blinds and make it as dark as you can. Then you will really be able to see the beam of light coming out of that thing.

Well, many blacks, Hispanics and other minorities in this country are living in poverty; in areas where their lives and the lives of their families are in danger from crime—drive-by shootings and much more; in neighborhoods where drug-dealers and pimps are king. They are living in the darkness and they need the light! A committed ministry team of suburban Christians can be a bright light in a crime-ridden area of the inner city.

I hope nobody misunderstands what I am saying. I am not saying that the people who live in inner-city areas are any less Christian than those who live in the suburbs. My own experience is that if you go into the poorest, most hopeless ghetto, you often find some of the dearest, sweetest, strongest Christian people on the planet. But all too often they have few marketable skills, little in the way of education and, try as hard as they might, no knowledge of how to go about changing their neighborhood.

That is why they need light from the outside. They need the skills and training that white suburban Christians can bring to them. They need assistance from people who will see them as equals and partners and who are willing to demonstrate that partnership by relocating into the community.

What they do not need, as Tom pointed out, is some detached outsider standing back and telling them in a condescending way how to do things. This is not a one-way street, you see, and it is most definitely not a superior-inferior relationship.

If you are a white Christian who decides to relocate to the inner city, have the attitude that you are going to receive from the people there as well as give to them. I cannot tell you how many times white Christians have told me that they tried to help, but that the people they were trying to reach out to did not seem to want their help. When I looked closely at the situation, I could see why they did not want it—because of how it was presented. The help was all wrapped up in an attitude like this: "Here I am, stooping down to help you people. I know what's best for you, so listen to me and I'll show you how it's done."

Minorities welcome an attitude of a different sort: "I'd like to share with you some of my knowledge and skills, but I expect to learn from you, too. Tell me what you need, and then let's work together to find a way to meet it."

There is one more attitude the residents of the inner city do not want—a suggestion that "I'm going to teach you so that you can move out of this place, and maybe get a nice new home in the suburbs." It is good to want to help someone like that, I agree. But it is far better to work together toward making his or her neighborhood a better place.

What happens most of the time is that as soon as a person from the inner city gets a better education or a better job, he moves out. That means that those who remain in the inner city are the ones who do not have decent educations or the skills necessary to get good jobs. It also means that life in the inner city will never get better—that those mostly minority neighborhoods will remain centers of unemployment, poverty and crime.

Your relocating to the inner city, on the other hand, is an important step you and your ministry team can take to help change conditions there. Think about it this way: If you belong to a church that sends missionaries overseas, why not consider sending some missionaries to the inner city?

Perhaps there are four or five families from your church who would agree to relocate, and could actually be supported in their mission work in the minority neighborhood. They could join forces with a black or Hispanic church, worship with those brothers and sisters, put their money into the collection plate there and be partners with the people. It could be the beginning of a mutually beneficial relationship between two churches—a relatively affluent suburban congregation and a relatively poor urban congregation.

I have to say once again, though, because of past history, that I am not talking about a rich church in the suburbs taking over a poor church in the city. I am talking about a relationship between two churches whose people aim to get to know one another, learn to love one another and get to the point of sharing one another's burdens the way Scripture commands, so that all the gifts God has given the various members of the two churches are being used for the edification and benefit of everyone.

Relocation is a big, big step. But I wish that America's biggest churches would come to see this country's minority neighborhoods as every bit as important a mission field as, say, Africa or Asia. If that happened, I am convinced it would go a long way toward bringing about racial reconciliation in this country.

That brings us to the second of the two R's:

2. Reconciliation

Reconciliation is the aim of this book and the central theme of the Gospel.

One of the first Bible verses any child learns is John 3:16. I love that verse because it tells in a few words what the Gospel is all about: "For God so loved the world that He gave His only begotten Son, that whoever believes in Him should not perish but have everlasting life."

That verse summarizes the amazing story of reconciliation through God's love—a theme repeated numerous times throughout the Scriptures. Romans 5:10–11, for example, says:

> For if when we were enemies we were reconciled to God through the death of His Son, much more, having been reconciled, we shall be saved by His life. And not only that, but we also rejoice in God through our Lord Jesus Christ, through whom we have now received the reconciliation.

And Colossians 1:21–22:

> And you, who once were alienated and enemies in your mind by wicked works, yet now He has reconciled in the body of His flesh through death, to present you holy, and blameless, and irreproachable in His sight. . . .

Finally, 2 Corinthians 5:18–19 tells us that we, too, need to be involved in the work of reconciliation:

> Now all things are of God, who has reconciled us to Himself through Jesus Christ, and has given us the ministry of reconciliation, that is, that God was in Christ reconciling the world to Himself, not imputing their trespasses to them, and has committed to us the word of reconciliation.

Most of us, I am sure, understand what these verses are talking about. But for the sake of anyone who may not be clear on the subject, let me explain.

Sin had tainted the creation. And because God is holy and righteous and cannot allow human unholiness and unrighteousness in His presence, human beings were separated from God. God, being all-wise, saw that the only way mankind could be reconciled to Him was through the death of Jesus Christ, His sinless Son made man. For it was only through appropriating the righteousness of Christ that sinful man would be able to come back into God's presence.

Isn't it amazing that God loved us so much He was willing to sacrifice His only Son as the means of reconciliation? Isn't it amazing that Jesus Christ loved us so much that He was willing to go to the cross in order to reconcile us to the Father?

When some people think of this amazing act of reconciliation, they think of it in historical terms. Somewhere 'way back in the mists of time, mankind turned his back on God, so God acted, through the death and resurrection of Christ, to bridge the gap between Himself and the people He created.

This is true, of course. But when I refer to people needing to be reconciled to God, I am not talking about the distant past but about the here and now—about you and me and everyone who is alive today. The sad truth is, we have all turned away from God. We have all been separated by our sins from Him. And we all need the reconciliation provided by the blood of Christ. In fact, we need that means of reconciliation not only once but many times. Even the most sincere, well-meaning Christian will slip, trip and stumble. But whenever that happens, the door of reconciliation is always open, thanks to the sacrifice God made on our behalf.

Looking at God's amazing love and gift as an example, two things about reconciliation are immediately apparent:

It is vitally important.
It is an ongoing process.

We can see by the value God placed on it that reconciliation is important. If He went to such extraordinary lengths to reconcile us to Himself, how can we not go to extraordinary lengths to reconcile our brothers and sisters to us? God expects us to value our brothers and sisters the way He does. He expects us to reach across racial and cultural boundaries to love them and be reconciled to them. I see it not as an option, but as an integral part of the Gospel.

I also see reconciliation as something that takes time. The divisions in our country are deep ones. We have deep wounds that have not yet begun to heal. We have hurts and resentments that have never been dealt with. It will require time, patience and perseverance to overcome these obstacles to reconciliation.

One more thing about reconciliation. Anyone who wants to be an agent of reconciliation must be willing to put himself completely into the effort. It cannot be done in a halfhearted way or with an attitude that says, "Well, I've done my part, so now it's up to the other guy."

I am sure you have heard it said that any marriage in which both partners try to meet each other halfway is doomed. Maybe it is a cliché, but there is a lot of truth in clichés. What this one means is that for any marriage to work, both partners must be willing to give one hundred percent—not grudgingly but out of love and concern for the other partner. The truth is, the husband who thinks he is giving one hundred percent is probably giving somewhere around fifty percent. The same is true of the wife. So when you have two people putting everything they have into their marriage, they are probably meeting each other somewhere near the middle.

We human beings are so self-oriented that it is easy for us to magnify our own contributions and underestimate how much the other guy is giving.

Are you willing to give one hundred percent when it comes to reconciliation? Jesus Christ did.

That brings us to the third R:

3. Redistribution

When I mention redistribution, some people get upset. They start telling me that I am talking like a Communist, and they say it is not fair to take things from the rich and redistribute them to the poor.

But that is not the kind of redistribution I am talking about. What I mean by redistribution is helping give the poor the skills they need to succeed in life. When I think about redistribution, I see in my mind a skilled white person working with minority children to give them the tools and incentives to make something of their lives.

Go into almost any inner city in the United States and you will find an area where the majority of kids (almost all of them black or Hispanic) never graduate from high school. You will find kids being drawn into drug-dealing, prostitution and other kinds of criminal behavior because they do not have the skills to do anything else. They need foundational skills and qualities that will enable them to go out in the world and possess it.

Take a look at your life and ask yourself what skills you have that you could share with some minority person from a disadvantaged background. A white plumber could take a young black or Hispanic person under his wing and teach him or her the tools of his trade. A carpenter could do the same; so could a businessman or businesswoman. Whatever skills you possess, there is someone who can learn from you. Most of the marketable skills in this country can be found in the white community, and they need to be spread around. That is what I mean by redistribution—bringing the disenfranchised into the mainstream of American society.

I look at it this way (and you have heard it before): Give a man a fish and you have fed him once. Teach him how to fish, and pretty soon he will own the whole pond.

To me, it would be a dream come true to see the members of a large suburban church (or the members of many large suburban churches) get excited about redistribution. It would work the same way the Peace Corps works, except that it would all happen right here at home in the U.S.

Just think of the changes that would take place in the inner city! People would acquire skills. They would be able to get good jobs. They would learn how to save and invest their money back into the community. The kids would learn how to develop and control the means of production, not so they could move out to the suburbs and have a better life there, but so they could bring the better life into their communities.

I said earlier that there is nothing we can do to change America's past. But there is plenty we can do—with God's help—to change her future.

And it is time we got started.

A Final Word 15

John Perkins

I have been hurt in many different ways by racial alienation, but I especially remember one incident that involved my son Phillip. Perhaps it was not that big a deal, but it really hurt me because I knew how much it hurt Phillip.

We were living in Mendenhall at the time. Phillip was no more than eight or nine years old, and he became good buddies with a little white boy about the same age. They had a good time together—playing ball, climbing trees, wrestling, doing all the things little boys do.

Then one day the other boy came over to our house to tell Phillip that he was sorry, but he couldn't play with him anymore. The other white kids were making fun of him because he was playing with Phillip, and he just could not take the teasing.

I remember Phillip telling the other little boy that he shouldn't let other people destroy their friendship.

"I want you to be my friend," he said.

But the other little guy would not listen. He said he was sorry, but that was just the way it was.

And he never played with Phillip again.

I have not talked to Phillip about that incident in quite a while. I am not even sure if he remembers it. But I remember it—and I always will. In some ways, as I think back on it now, it hurts me even more than it did all those years ago. That is probably because back then I had a lot of anger mixed in with my pain. The anger has long since faded away, but the pain is still there.

You know, I cannot blame an eight-year-old boy for not being willing to take a stand. After all, he was only a child. But I am not a child. You are not a child. So I am saying to you now that I want *you* to be my friend. I want you to join me in my mission to destroy ignorance and racism. I am asking *you* to be willing to take a stand.

As we stand together, black and white, side by side, we will recognize that Christ has one Church, and the love that flows from that truth will ignite the flame that can burn away racism and bigotry.

Tom Tarrants

As the children's song says, "Red and yellow, black and white, they are precious in His sight."

Christ died for *all* people. His love encompasses every color, national origin, language and culture. If Jesus loved us so much that He was willing to die for us, how can we not be willing to set aside our racial and cultural differences and learn to love one another?

Again, there are many things we can do, if only we are willing, to be agents of reconciliation. I am convinced it is no accident that some of us have white skin while others have black skin or skin of another color. God made us that way because it provides an opportunity for us to demonstrate the power of His love to overcome our differences. It gives us a chance to demonstrate that we can work together for His glory and the good of all. And it shows how much we all need each other.

Benjamin Franklin reminded his fellow colonists that "we must all hang together, or assuredly we shall all hang separately" as traitors against the British crown. Those words are urgently true today. Much rides on our ability to get together. At stake is not only the future of our country, but the future of many precious souls for whom Christ died.

When the unconverted person looks at us as followers of Christ, does he see people divided along racial lines, people who are angry and hostile toward one another? If he does, then who can blame him if he turns away from us and rejects our message of Christ's love and grace?

If, on the other hand, he sees that we are people who sincerely love one another and are working at overcoming our differences—if our actions square with our proclamation of Christ's love—then he will have to take our message seriously.

Much, much more than the future of our country is at stake. Indeed, the credibility of the Gospel and the future of the American Church hang in the balance.